THE
Power
OF ONE
CHRIST-LIKE
LIFE

Contents

Preface

This is not so much a preface as it is an open letter to those who suppose I am ignoring the world's sins. By the time you have completed this book, you will have discovered why I cannot side with those who are judging and condemning their nations. It is not that I disagree with their analysis of what is wrong, for the world has truly entered a phase of deepened deception and darkness. My disagreement centers on the way we, as Christians, deal with the evil in our world.

Before I explain my position, let me first familiarize you with my past. I have wept, probably more than most, over the sins of my nation, the United States. I'm not glossing over the insidious iniquity that seems to continually attach its tendrils around American culture. I am troubled when I hear of Christians, especially pastors, who make a practice of watching movies in which sex, gratuitous violence, and foul language are part of the "entertainment." I don't feel prudish at all when I say that I am offended by the sexually blatant magazine covers at checkout counters. I hate dirty jokes; crude humor is an offense to me.

I despise racial jokes and ethnic slurs. In fact, I am ashamed before God for the history of poor race relations in America and that whites, of which I am one, have taken so long to repent of their attitudes.

This is a charge against my country for which I have positioned myself in ongoing prayer, repentance, and action before God.

I don't want you to think that I am unburdened or ignorant of the wholesale cheapening of life in our world, whether it manifests itself through marital conflicts or abortion or gangs or with child abuse or murder. I remain horrified by the multiplied tragedies of war. I'm not aloof from these things, not in the least. I have fasted over them, prayed about them, wept concerning them, and been, at times, sick because of them. I know that it was largely because of mankind's violence that God destroyed the world during Noah's day. My soul is afflicted with the wounding of mankind. I am deeply aware of these things.

When homosexual agendas, witchcraft, New Age cults, "Christian" cults, atheism, or paganism are promoted for any reason, it disturbs me greatly. When I see my tax money misspent on worthless pork-barrel projects while vast multitudes of little children are abandoned to a hellish, inner-city existence, my soul burns within me. I believe we need to speak out, to warn and to weep, concerning all these things.

I am deeply grieved over the divisions, selfish ambitions, slanders, immoralities, prayerlessness, and worldliness that exist in Christianity. I lament that, more often than not, the church has not been an example of righteousness and true holiness to the world.

Indeed, many things have distressed me about the sin in my world. So, if you are concerned about sin, I am as well. I have spoken out against all these things and will continue to do so. We are united and in agreement concerning the reality of sin and how it destroys the human soul.

But I have not just been troubled; I have been involved in trying to change my world. In the past, my two oldest children and I have been arrested for protesting abortion. I have published pro-life letters in newspapers and pleaded directly with abortion providers.

Long before *race relations* became a recognizable term, I organized a regional reconciliation service between people of color and whites at our city hall. I brought together news reporters and television crews, mayors, police chiefs, and church and community leaders from various backgrounds throughout eastern Iowa. We covenanted with God and our local political leaders that our city of Cedar Rapids, Iowa, would be a "city of refuge." I personally paid for it all. For many years now, I've been hosting similar reconciliation services throughout scores of cities in the United States, Canada, and other nations where racial prejudice has left people divided and oppressed.

Regarding the church in America, not too many have done more to help unite Christians than I. In hundreds of cities, with thousands of pastors, I have led citywide meetings with no other goal than to humble ourselves in repentance and prayer and return to biblical, Christ-centered unity. I long to see the Lord's prayer for oneness among His people fulfilled. (See John 17:20–21.)

I'm not telling you these things to boast, but to assure you that what I have to say about God's heart toward our nations is not being written by a theorist or philosopher far removed from such pressing issues as these. Let me say it again: I believe the church needs to confront sin and injustice. If we fail to speak the truth in love (Eph. 4:15) to those who promote wickedness, their blood, according to God's Word, will be upon our heads. (See Ezekiel 33:7–9.)

However, throughout my struggle, I have not only been made aware of America's sinfulness, I also have simultaneously been discovering something about the Almighty. What I have found is not just theological information; it's revelation concerning His heart: God's *"mercy triumphs over judgment"* (James 2:13). The Lord is good. He is slow to anger and abundant in lovingkindness (Ps. 103:8); He has shown that He will relent concerning calamity (Jer. 18:8), if He can find but one Christlike person praying for mercy. (See Genesis 18:20–32.)

Thus, my deepest prayer is that, by the time you complete this book, your vision will have been restored to seeing our most powerful weapon in our fight against evil: the grace and love of God. My plea before the Father is that new hope and courage will be granted to you. Most importantly, I pray that your soul will perfectly match the pattern of Christ's, who ever lives to make intercession (Heb. 7:25) and who stands before the throne of God as a Lamb slain for sin (Rev. 5:6).

—Francis Frangipane

Introduction

I am an American, and the state of the American church is especially important to me. Since 1989, some remarkable advances have been made in the church in the United States. We have seen a genuine beginning toward reconciliation between denominations and races. The prayer movement has simply exploded, with tens of millions of Christians serving God in various intercessory expressions. Prayer has expanded from quiet and intimate to loud and passionate; prayer ministries have taken to the streets and squares of our cities, with nearly a million and a half men repenting at our nation's capital. Additionally, many leaders have adopted a fasting lifestyle, with great numbers embracing forty-day fasts for America's healing.

As a result, violent crime has dropped in the United States to the lowest levels since statistics on this subject have been kept and analyzed. Divorce, abortion, teen pregnancies, and a host of other problems have, in varying degrees, also been declining. The best news is that, in a number of places, revival and renewal are beginning to bring multitudes face-to-face with the living God.

As Christians, we know we still need to make more progress in these areas before God is satisfied. Most of us who are guiding the church in America have reasons to be encouraged. However, in recent months I have watched a disturbing trend in the American church: multitudes of "Bible-believing" Christians have turned angry toward the world for its sins. Anger has led to bitterness and begun to replace redemptive, intercessory prayer with calls for judgment. Stark unbelief concerning America and the possibility of revival has begun to invade the souls of certain leaders; a dark hopelessness concerning the future is settling upon a growing number of Christians.

My goal is to counter hopelessness with vision. I have written this book to dispel the darkness of fear and unbelief and to position each of us, no matter what nation we are from or how evil it seems, at the throne of God's great mercy. My intention is not only to defend what God has begun in the church, but also to empower us to fulfill the vision of Christlikeness.

Just as I have faith for America, I also believe that God is about to awaken many nations. In fact, He has already begun to do so in many places in South and Central America, Africa, and Asia. These are all places that a few years ago no one predicted would experience harvest or revival. Because I see the Lord moving mightily in these other lands, I passionately believe that it is not too late for your country as well. How can I say that? Simply because *you* are there.

The power of even one Christlike intercessor can delay God's wrath until the time comes when He pours out His mercy. As long as you don't give up on your land, I believe God will not abandon it either. Indeed, it is my passionate, unbending conviction that the prayer of a Christlike intercessor is the most powerful force in the universe. To illustrate this point, I have included many examples of the power of one Christlike life. The future belongs to the Christlike.

One

The Divine Obsession

There are three basic categories of Christians. The largest group are those who perceive the world's sin and corruption and consider it impossible to change. They evaluate their spiritual capabilities and conclude that they are nearly powerless to transform the world around them. Unable to cope, they retreat into what seems to be a shelter of apathy. Yet most are not truly apathetic, for their souls, like Lot's (see 2 Peter 2:7–8), inwardly grieve at the conduct of unprincipled men around them. Without spiritual resources, however, their flame has diminished to the size of their immediate family and needs.

The second class of Christians consists of those who would rather rail at the storm of evil than hide from it. Though smaller in number than the first, they are by no means apathetic; in fact, they appear exactly opposite. They rage at the depravity of the ungodly and protest the audacity of the wicked. They pound pulpits and sidewalks; they are both vocal and visible. Yet their ability to effect positive societal change has been, for the most part, neutralized by their negativity and rage. They are characterized and then dismissed as judgmental extremists. Sinners cannot endure the harshness of their approach.

Both groups sincerely desire to see our culture transformed. Yet the same problem afflicts them: they are troubled that the world is unchristian, without being troubled that their own hearts are un-Christlike. They do not perceive the priority of God's heart, which is the transformation of the church into the image of Christ.

WORLD CHANGERS NEEDED

It is this very passion to be conformed to Christ that separates the third group from the others. Though smallest in number, its members are the most effective. Throughout history, these have been the world changers. These have understood the priority of God. They know that the Father's highest passion is to behold His Son revealed in a believer's soul. As much as they are moved with compassion for the lost, their primary quest is not to touch their neighbors' hearts, but to touch the heart of God. They know if they awaken the Father's pleasure, the power of His Spirit will go before them. God Himself will change the hearts of those around them.

It is my mission to isolate and exalt the power of the Christlike life. My goal in this book is to unveil the influence one such person has to awaken the pleasure of God. Between chapters, I will present profiles of individuals whose yielded lives so pleased God that He empowered them to change nations. As He transformed them into the image of Christ, they, in turn, transformed nations for Christ.

TO BE LIKE CHRIST

Indeed, it was this quest for Christlikeness that was the secret of Paul's success. He wrote, *"That I may know Him, and the power of His resurrection and the fellowship of His sufferings, being conformed to His death"* (Phil. 3:10).

Paul's passion was taken up with this one primary goal: *"being conformed"* to the life purpose of Jesus Christ. The apostle's quest was not to win the world, but to know Christ Jesus, his Lord. The works Paul accomplished—founding churches, writing half the New Testament, demonstrating miraculous spiritual gifts, and remaining faithful throughout times of terrible suffering—were all incidental to the fulfillment of his passion to know Christ.

Likewise with us, the Father's immediate, primary goal is a church in conformity to Christ. He desires this end even more than seeing a world in revival. Indeed, if salvation of the lost were the Almighty's immediate priority, He would simply bypass the church and save men Himself. Has He not demonstrated, as seen in Paul's conversion, that His abilities to do this are without limit? Yet He has chosen most often not to reveal Himself in His irresistible splendor, but through the transformation of our humanity.

This, my friends, is the glorious mystery of our existence: the Almighty has purposed from eternity to create a race of men who, though tested in a corrupt and violent world, bear the image and likeness of Christ. (See Genesis 1:27.) Christ calls this heavenly-natured people, the church, His *"new creation"* (2 Cor. 5:17 NKJV).

THE HOLY OBSESSION

To be obsessed is "to think about something un-
ceasingly." In this sense, the Father is obsessed with
filling the universe with the Spirit of His Son, Jesus
Christ. Beginning with eternity past, revealing the
Firstborn in the womb of time, and continuing with
the transformation of the church, the Father desires
all creation ultimately to be summed up in Christ
(Eph. 1:10). Our goal is to participate in His purpose
in *"the summing up"* (v. 10) of our lives in Christ.

Therefore, in these pages, we will examine what
it means to be Christ-like. We will look at why the
Father tolerates an evil world and how He desires to
use it in the perfection of our lives. We will study the
nature of redemptive intercession and, in awe of the
love of God, behold why redemption so stirs the Father's heart.

Besides the titled theme, *The Power of One
Christlike Life,* there is another underlying principle
that will be repeated throughout this book: *"Mercy
triumphs over judgment"* (James 2:13). In my esti-
mation, this companion truth embodies the heart
and purpose of Jesus Christ. To know it at the core
of our actions engenders great confidence. Indeed, it
is to discover that the Father is not seeking opportunities to destroy us, but reasons to pour out His
mercy.

True, His mercy springs forth most often purely
from His own initiative. However, at other times, He
seeks to produce within us Christlike conditions of
the heart, which precipitate the moving of His redemptive power. It is here, in the transformation of

our lives, that we discover and fulfill the wondrous obsession of God: the unveiling of His Son in the earth. It is here, at the threshold of Christ in us, that we discover the power one Christlike life has upon the heart of God.

Father, let my heart become as obsessed with Your Son as You are. Let the fullness of my absorption with Him displace all other pursuits until, at the mere glimpse of Jesus, my whole being is flooded with the pleasure You Yourself feel.

The Power of One Christlike Life...

Saint Patrick
b. circa 390 A.D., Scotland
d. circa 461 A.D., Downpatrick, County Down, Ireland

Saint Patrick

*L*egend and historical fact intertwine to create the portrait of Saint Patrick, who is credited with turning a whole country from idolatry to Christianity. Although accounts of his illustrating the mystery of the Trinity by using the sacred plant of the Druids, the shamrock, or ridding Ireland of snakes may be debated, his love for the Gospel, which ignited his missionary zeal, is indisputable.

At sixteen years of age, Patrick, the son of a nobleman, was captured from his homeland in Britain by a band of pirates and taken to Ireland. He was sold to Milchu, a cruel master and pagan warlord. Like the Prodigal Son, Patrick remembered better days. Who would have thought that the cherished son of a nobleman would be tending cattle and swine? The seeds of truth that he had been taught but had not embraced now found receptive soil in his heart. Later in life he would write of this time, "The love and the fear of God and faith increased so much, and the spirit of prayer so grew within me, that I often prayed an hundred times in the day....The Spirit was burning within me." Captivity became a fertile training ground for his future mission.

After six years of slavery, Patrick heard a voice in his dreams, telling him, "Behold, the ship is ready for you." He escaped and miraculously journeyed home.

Patrick's family begged him never to leave them again, but the calling of his heavenly Father to return to Ireland had to be obeyed. Forsaking comfort, Patrick was compelled to bring Christ's love to those who had once been his captors. The language of Ireland and the knowledge of Druidic practices that he had learned while enslaved now served him as he preached.

Patrick used a pagan feast day to demonstrate God's power over heathen darkness. All over Ireland, fires were to be extinguished until a signal blaze was lit by Druidic priests at Tara, the seat of the kings, where the chieftains of Ireland had gathered.

On the hill of Slane opposite the valley from Tara, Patrick lit a fire to celebrate the resurrection of Christ. The Druids warned King Laoghaire that the fire would "blaze for ever in this land unless it be this very night extinguished." Repeated efforts were made to put out the fire and to kill the one who had ignited it. The Druids and magicians used all of their black magic and occult powers, but they had no effect on the one who represented the all-powerful God.

As a result, Laoghaire, supreme monarch of Ireland, gave Patrick permission to preach his faith throughout the land. The sacred fire of evangelism burned brightly, dispelling the darkness of paganism.

During his thirty years as Bishop of Ireland, Patrick dedicated 350 bishops, established at least 300 churches, baptized over 120,000 Irishmen, and set up numerous schools and monasteries. After his death, it would be the Irish who would return as missionaries to Scotland, England, France, Belgium, and Germany.

An excerpt from Patrick's prayer for deliverance that is said to have been composed as he made his way to confront the Druids at Tara reveals the faith of this saint who fought the powers of darkness to bring Christ's light to the Emerald Isle:

> Christ, as a light,
> Illumine and guide me!
> Christ, as a shield, o'ershadow and cover me!

Christ, be under me! Christ, be over me!
Christ, be beside me,
On left hand and right!
Christ, be before me, behind me, about me!
Christ, this day be within and without me!

Two

Mercy Triumphs over Judgment

For whom He foreknew, He also predestined to
become conformed to the image of His Son, that He
might be the first-born among many brethren.
—Romans 8:29

Functional Christlikeness is the singular goal of
God for the church, yet we find instead that
many Christians are angry. Why shouldn't they be,
they ask. Major strongholds of evil and oppression
exist almost without restraint in our society today.
Not only is evil expanding in our culture, but many
of its forms are actually protected by a demonically
invaded legal system.

Their anger is understandable. Whether we re-
side in a major metropolitan area or make our home
in a small rural setting, the boundaries of morality
in our country continue to erode. We have only to
think about the protection given to those favoring
abortion, the mainstreaming of homosexuality, or
the applause offered to immorality, and a holy
grieving stirs within us.

REDEMPTION, NOT ANGER

We should be deeply troubled by sin, for it has the power not only to destroy our souls, but also to provoke the wrath of God upon our nation. Yet how we handle evil in our society is the point of this study. Our goal is to win our war—not just react to the battle. We must remember:

> *We wrestle not against flesh and blood, but against principalities, against powers, against the rulers of the darkness of this world, against spiritual wickedness in high places.*
>
> (Eph. 6:12 KJV)

The moment our anger is directed toward *"flesh and blood"* enemies, we surrender our hope for victory. God's objective goes beyond simply eliminating evil. He seeks redemption, not revenge.

We might have all the doctrines correct about salvation, and our church attendance record might be spotless, but if we continue to harbor an angry spirit, we are walking away from Christlikeness; we are in danger of falling away.

Yet you are not in apostasy, beloved. Your quest is the nature of Christ. You know that apart from conformity to Him, you will never be satisfied. Though we all have often fallen short, still we abide beneath our Father's covering grace. Indeed, so essential to His purpose is the Christlike transformation of our hearts, that God will endure our frequent mistakes, granting us time until His call to love awakens within us.

Thus, with relief we read how the early disciples, who similarly misrepresented Christ's redemptive mission, eventually were restored and transformed. When Jesus and His followers passed through Samaria, they were rejected and scorned by the locals. Offended, the apostles became indignant and angry. Two disciples even asked, *"Lord, do You want us to command fire to come down from heaven and consume them?"* (Luke 9:54).

How eager they were to embrace the administration of God's wrath! How conveniently the wrath of God could be used to support their own shortsighted love. Jesus rebuked them plainly, saying, *"You do not know what kind of spirit you are of"* (v. 55).

This is exactly the problem in Christianity today: many sincere Christians do not know what spirit they are of. They do not know the difference between a judgmental spirit and the Spirit of Christ, the Redeemer.

In the clearest terms, Jesus again explained His mission to His disciples. He said, *"The Son of Man did not come to destroy men's lives, but to save them"* (v. 56).

Jesus was speaking of all men in general, but His response concerned cultural enemies in particular. The Samaritans, in the minds of the Jews, were a people scorned and reproached. Yet, even for people who were enemies, He said that He did not come to destroy but to save. His disciples eventually learned this lesson and were used by God to spread the Gospel all over the world.

What we see in Jesus is to be repeated in substance and power in the church. Thus, our mission is to carry out His mission: to see people and situations redeemed, not destroyed.

LOVE, NOT LAW

Yet, for some reason, many Christians identify the height of spirituality not with Christ but with Israel's Old Testament prophets, who were called by God to bring specific messages of warning and punishment to His people. Christian, listen to me: we are not Old Testament prophets; we are new covenant redeemers. Our primary pattern is not Jeremiah, but Jesus Christ, who brought grace and truth into the world (John 1:17). Our standard is love, not law. Love is the fulfillment of the law (Rom. 13:10). We are the body of Christ. While we can learn much from the Old Testament, and see reflections of Christ in it, we have no purpose greater than to reveal Christ as He revealed Himself in the New Testament, as the fulfillment of the law.

Why should we pattern ourselves after Israel's prophets when they had specific messages from God for specific circumstances? They were sent to a people under law, who did not have available Christ as Savior, and who did not know the indwelling of the Holy Spirit or the full grace of God, which is now available to all sinners. Under the law, if the Jews violated just one commandment, they were guilty of all (James 2:10). Although the Lord deeply loved the Israelites, they fell short of God's glory. However, the Father's purpose was not to condemn them, but to provide a better salvation, the free gift of eternal life through faith in Christ—redemption based not on what a man achieved, but on whom he believed.

"For God has shut up all in disobedience that He might show mercy to all" (Rom. 11:32). The prophet's exposure of Israel's sin was part of the closure of the old covenant, a preparation for God's people to embrace mercy. To pattern ourselves after the prophets is to position ourselves in a former dispensation under specific circumstances for which we have no involvement or voice.

Yet the disciples were emerging from the Old Testament dispensation. So when they sought to call fire upon their enemies, as appropriate as this seemed to them, Jesus corrected them. He did not come to destroy His enemies, but *"to save them"* (Luke 9:56).

"But," you argue, "God needs to judge sinners for what they are doing." That may be so. Perhaps the world needs a good dose of the wrath of God to wake it up. However, only One person in heaven and earth is worthy to initiate God's wrath: the Lamb who was slain, who stands in intercession before God's throne. (See Revelation 5:6–14.)

THE LAMB, NOT THE PROPHETS

Consider this: the only Being in all the universe worthy to release wrath because of sin is the very One in all the universe least likely to do so, since He Himself is the sacrifice for sin. The Lamb of God, whose offering abides eternally at God's throne, is the One to whom authority is given to open the book of divine wrath.

Jesus is the Lamb, the sacrifice for sin. Because He paid the highest price for redemption, we can be confident that He will not release divine fury until He fully exhausts divine mercy. Even then, when His judgments finally come, they will continue to be guided by His motive of mercy, giving time for sinners to repent.

God's Word tells us plainly: *"As He is, so also are we in this world"* (1 John 4:17). Our pattern is not the prophets, but the Lamb. Our goal is not merely the exposure of sin, but also the unveiling of the sacrifice for sin. Our great commission is to bring healing and the message of God's mercy to the nations. Until Christ breaks the seals that lead to wrath, we must stand in intercession before God as ambassadors of the Lamb.

May the Lord give us a clear vision of this truth: intercession is the essence of Christ's life. Not only is He now at the right hand of the Father interceding for us (Rom. 8:34), but His coming to earth and dying for sins was one extended act of intercession. Jesus beheld the depravity of mankind's sin. He examined it carefully in all of its offensiveness, perversity, and repulsiveness. But the wonder of the Gospel is that, in spite of mankind's sin, God so deeply loved the world that He sent His Son to die for us (John 3:16–17). We are called to follow this same amazing pattern of mercy.

We are not minimizing sin when we maximize Christ's mercy. There is a difference between whitewashing sin and bloodwashing it. The reality that compels God's heart, that is an underlying principle of life, is *"mercy triumphs over judgment"* (James 2:13). To live a life of mercy corresponds perfectly with God's heart. Mercy precisely fulfills the divine purpose: to transform man into the Redeemer's image.

IDENTIFIED WITH SINNERS

Throughout His life, Jesus reached out to people who were rejected by others. He loved those who were despised, scorned, and excluded. Yet His practice of dining with known evildoers offended the Pharisees, and they confronted Jesus' disciples with this question: *"Why is your Teacher eating with the tax-gatherers and sinners?"* (Matt. 9:11). When Jesus heard the question, He answered,

> *It is not those who are healthy who need a physician, but those who are sick. But go and learn what this means, "I DESIRE COMPASSION, AND NOT SACRIFICE," for I did not come to call the righteous, but sinners.*
>
> (Matt. 9:12–13)

COMPASSION, NOT SACRIFICE

He told the self-righteous to go and learn what God meant when He said, *"I DESIRE COMPASSION* [mercy], *AND NOT SACRIFICE."* A religion without love is an abomination to God. The church needs to learn that God desires love and compassion, not merely an adherence to ritual and sacrifice. Thus, Jesus said His Father's house would be a *"HOUSE OF PRAYER FOR ALL THE NATIONS"* (Mark 11:17). True prayer is born of love and comes in the midst of sin and need. It comes not to condemn, but to cover.

All nations sin. All cultures have seasons of moral decline and spiritual malaise. Yet these periods can become turning points if, in times of distress, intercessors cry to God for mercy. Thus, Christlike prayer brings redemption out of disaster.

MERCY, NOT WRATH

The church is created not to fulfill God's wrath, but to complete His mercy. Remember, we are called to be a *"HOUSE OF PRAYER FOR ALL...NATIONS."* Consider passionately this phrase: *"prayer for."* Jesus taught His disciples to *"pray for"* (Matt. 5:44) those who would persecute or mistreat them. When Job *"prayed for"* (Job 42:10) his friends, God fully restored him. We are to ***pray for*** *the peace of Jerusalem"* (Ps. 122:6, emphasis added), and *"pray for"* (James 5:16) each other so that we may be healed. Paul wrote that God desires all men to be saved (1 Tim. 2:4). Therefore, he urged *"that entreaties and prayers...be made on behalf of all men, for kings and all who are in authority"* (vv. 1–2).

INTERCESSION, NOT CYNICISM

"But," you argue, "my country (or city) is a modern manifestation of ancient Babylon."

I don't think so. But even if it were, when the Lord exiled Israel to Babylon, He didn't order His people to judge and criticize their new cities. Rather, He commanded, *"Seek the welfare of the city where I have sent you...and pray to the LORD on its behalf; for in its welfare you will have welfare"* (Jer. 29:7).

Time after time, the scriptural command is to pray *for,* not *against;* to pray *mercifully,* not *vindictively.* God's call is for prayer moved by compassion, not condemnation. Indeed, at its very essence, the nature of intercession is to appeal to God for forgiveness, and then redemption, to come to sinful people.

We have studied what is wrong with our society and can prove, with charts and surveys, the trends of sin, yet we have failed to appreciate the influence of the intercessions of Christ. We consider ourselves experts on the nature and cause of sin, but deny the nature and cause of Christ, which is redemption. My friends, being informed by the news media is in no way the same thing as being transformed into the nature of the Savior.

The media sees what is wrong with the world and exposes it; Christ saw what was wrong and died for it. If one could gaze into the image being created within the heart of the church, one would find that it would be more the cynical attitude of the news media than the redemptive attitude of our Shepherd. Righteousness must ascend higher than ascribing to the moral views of our political party; we are called to the standards of God.

Study Isaiah 53. It reveals in wondrous detail the Savior's nature: Christ numbered Himself with the sinners (v. 12). He interceded for the transgressors (v. 12). He is *"with us"* (see, for example, Matthew 1:23, emphasis added) and *"for us"* (Rom. 8:31, emphasis added), even when He is speaking to us of our iniquity.

But the world sees a church with rocks in its hands, looking for adulterers and sinners. We have become the "church of the angry Christians." In the drama that is unfolding in the world today, we have not usually been playing the role of Christ, but more often the part of the Pharisees. Let us drop the rocks from our hands, then lift our hands, without wrath, in prayer to God (1 Tim. 2:8).

"PRAYER-MENTAL," NOT JUDGMENTAL

God does not want us to be judgmental; He wants us prayer-mental. As instinctively as we have judged people, we should pray for them instead. Today, countless Christians are angry with their elected officials. We say our anger is "righteous indignation." Really? Jesus expressed "righteous indignation" for, perhaps, a total of one hour during His recorded ministry. Once was for the hardness of people's hearts (Mark 3:5), another was for the hypocrisy of the Pharisees and scribes (Matt. 23:13–36), and other times were at the temple when the Father's house was used for something other than redemptive prayer. (See, for example, Mark 11:17.) This is important: the thing that angered Jesus was not the sin in society, but the lack of love and intercession in His people.

How long has your anger lasted? Are you sure your love has not grown cold? Are you sure you are not seeking to justify a root of bitterness and call it righteous indignation?

"Well," some argue, "our government officials have sinned." When Paul called for prayer for kings in 1 Timothy 2:1–2, Nero was emperor of Rome. Nero was one of the most corrupt men who ever lived. He did not have an illicit relationship or two; he had public orgies. He skinned Christians alive. There were occasions when he illuminated his night banquets with living torches, Christians, who were tarred and then set ablaze on poles. Nero and his guests dined surrounded by Christians dying for their faith. Yet Paul wrote that we should pray *"for kings and all who are in authority"* (v. 2). Nero was king when Paul wrote this command.

Some may misread my words, assuming that I think there is nothing wrong in government or society. Yes, there are many things wrong in our world, and God will certainly call us, at various times, to confront the sins that plague our lands. However, my concern is not as much with the White House as with the Lord's house! If we are not praying for our elected officials, the least we can do is to stop cursing them! As it is written, *"YOU SHALL NOT SPEAK EVIL OF A RULER OF YOUR PEOPLE"* (Acts 23:5).

The Father's house is to be a house of prayer for kings and all in authority. We can adamantly disagree with the political views that a leader has, but we must also adamantly cry to God on their behalf and serve as intercessors, even for our cultural enemies.

I can understand the reason for anger toward elected officials, especially if we consider that they are not doing their jobs. But if all we do is judge them, we are not doing *our* jobs. It is not the Holy Spirit within us that calls for God to judge sinners; it is our frustration with people and the delay in the restoration of righteousness. My friend, beware; for when you pray for judgment to come, remember that it begins *"with the household of God"* (1 Pet. 4:17). To pray for God to judge a nation or city for its sins actually initiates judgment from God on the church for its sins! And the Almighty will start with those who are quickest to judge others!

When I pray for the political leaders guiding the United States, I ask the Lord to protect them from the influence of ungodly counselors. Where they have failed, I appeal to God to forgive them and to show mercy, in regard to the relaxed moral standards of our land and especially concerning abortion, which breaks the Lord's heart.

Yet I also acknowledge the good things the Lord has done through our national leaders; I am thankful to the Almighty for those things. Have our leaders done everything perfectly? No. But then, neither have we.

The Lord desires for us to *"stand in the gap"* (Ezek. 22:30), positioning ourselves between the failings of man and the sufficiency and forgiveness of God. Then, He calls us to persevere in this intercession until full transformation comes.

For all who are embittered with their nation's leaders, remember: each of us must give an account for our sins at the *"judgment seat of Christ"* (2 Cor. 5:10). Let us consider with holy fear the warning of God: *"Judgment will be merciless to one who has shown no mercy; mercy triumphs over judgment"* (James 2:13).

Father, I ask You to forgive me for my lack of forgiveness toward our elected officials. Lord, I ask You to forgive, cleanse, and renew them in

Your mighty presence. Appear to them, Lord, in the night hours; save them from the lies and plans of hell. Touch and heal their families, and renew them as well in Your love. Lord, I ask You to forgive my harshness toward all who have offended me. O God, this day, deliver me from my judgmental attitudes! Help me to remember in all things and at all times that "mercy triumphs over judgment"!

The Power of One Christlike Life...

Count Nikolaus Ludwig von Zinzendorf
b. May 26, 1700, Dresden, Saxony, Germany
d. May 9, 1760, Herrnhut, Saxony, Germany

Count Nikolaus Ludwig von Zinzendorf

*T*o understand the impact of Count Zinzendorf's life, one must have some knowledge of the history of the Moravian church. The *Unitas Fratrum,* or the Unity of the Brethren, had its beginnings in 1457 among the followers of the Bohemian reformer John Huss (Jan Hus). Huss, a Roman Catholic priest, was burned at the stake for heresy on July 6, 1415. He believed that the Gospel should be preached in the vernacular rather than in Latin, that Communion should be available to all believers, and that the church should not sell indulgences. His followers looked to the Bible as their only standard of faith and established disciplines of purity, simplicity, and brotherly love based on the practices and teachings of the early apostolic church.

The *Unitas Fratrum* gained prominence in Bohemia, Moravia, and Poland, until their religious liberty was extinguished. Following the Thirty Years' War (1618–1648), Ferdinand II tried to impose the Roman Catholic faith on all his subjects. After one hundred years of religious persecution, Bohemian and Moravian descendents of the Brethren sought refuge in Saxony on the estate of Count Zinzendorf. There they founded Herrnhut, which means "The Lord's Watch," and worshiped in the Lutheran parish church in Berthelsdorf, a neighboring village.

Count Zinzendorf, a devout Pietist, was concerned with spiritual renewal within the Lutheran Church. Philipp Jakob Spener, a major Pietist theologian, as well as a close friend of the Zinzendorf family, proposed a "heart religion" rather than a "head religion." This emphasis on emotional experiences over creed and doctrine was one of the three general characteristics of Pietism, all of which were influential in Zinzendorf's life.

Emerging from this experiential emphasis was a focus on personal purity and benevolent actions. Both the poor at home and the heathen across the seas were important concerns for the Pietists. Finally, there was an emphasis on the priesthood of all believers. Laymen were urged to be as actively involved in Bible study and ministry as those with specific callings as ministers. Although Zinzendorf studied law at Wittenberg and took a post in the Saxon court, he soon took this teaching to heart and became involved with his new tenants at Herrnhut. In this way, Zinzendorf influenced the spiritual lives of both the Moravians and the Lutherans.

Zinzendorf followed the Spenerian teaching of developing little churches within the larger church, which would act as spiritual leavening to revitalize the Lutheran Church. This movement, called the *diaspora,* was a vital contribution of the Moravian church. Zinzendorf organized the Moravians at Herrnhut in choirs, grouping people according to age, gender, and marital status. He believed that "there can be no Christianity without community."

His concern for unity among the brethren caused Zinzendorf to urge the Moravians to settle the differences that were causing divisions among them. He led Bible studies and prayer meetings that culminated in the outpouring of the Holy Spirit during a Communion celebration in the Berthelsdorf Lutheran Church on August 13, 1727. Later Count Zinzendorf would say of that day, now considered the spiritual birthday of the Renewed Moravian Church, that the congregation stopped judging each other and recognized their own unworthiness to partake of the Lord's Supper. However, as they experienced their acceptance in the Beloved, their tears turned to joy and their misery to happiness.

Their desire to share this transforming experience motivated them the to take the Gospel to those who did not know of its life-changing power. The unity, love, and forgiveness experienced on that day swept away the conflicts that had been plaguing their community, and a renewed determination to work together in mission was born. The revival of 1727 began, and the "hourly intercession" was started. Twenty-four men and twenty-four women pledged to pray for one hour each day so that prayer would be continuous within their community. The number of adults praying grew, and even the children began a similar plan. For one hundred years, this ongoing prayer meeting was continued. In the first twenty-five years, over one hundred missionaries would go out from that community, supported by the prayers of their fellow believers. When John Wesley visited the community in 1738, he wrote in his journal, "I would gladly have spent my life here....Oh, when shall this Christianity cover the earth as water covers the sea?"

The work of the Moravians would expand. First, two missionaries were sent to the Dutch West Indies. Then the work spread to Greenland, Suriname, South Africa, Algiers, and to the North American Indians in Georgia. Moravian settlements were especially strong in Bethlehem, Nazareth, and Lititz, Pennsylvania.

Count Zinzendorf exemplifies what God can do through the influence of a devoted, praying man. The revival that started among the Moravians at Herrnhut ultimately spread to the far corners of the world.

Three

Grace and Truth

"When we preach on hell, we might at least do it
with tears in our eyes."
—Dwight L. Moody

I have been pleading Christ's case for a merciful church. How merciful should we expect to become? Jesus said, *"Be merciful, just as your Father is merciful"* (Luke 6:36). Here is what the Father did in His mercy: He sent His only begotten Son to die for our sins. We are to reach for nothing short of the nature of Christ who, instead of destroying His enemies, forgave and died for them.

At the same time, the living God does not withhold from us revelation of what we have done wrong, nor does He blind us to the sins of our society. Central to the mission of the Holy Spirit is bringing conviction to the *"world concerning sin, and righteousness, and judgment"* (John 16:8). If we are to be merciful, even as the Father is merciful, we must also be prepared to speak in defense of righteousness.

WARN AS AN ACT OF LOVE

Certainly there are times when we must warn loved ones, or even churches or cities, of the dire consequences of defying God's impending judgments. At the same time, we must do so without personal vindictiveness or wrath. There are times when we are called to proclaim from the rooftops the truths of God, no matter how hard the message God has given us, but such proclamations must not be judgmental or self-righteous.

The mercy of God is more truly served when we can say to one who has sinned, "What you have done is wrong, but God offers opportunities for redemption." When called to correct, we must learn how to present ourselves to sinners *"in a spirit of gentleness; each one looking to* [himself], *lest* [he] *too be tempted"* (Gal. 6:1).

Indeed, the redemption of God is ill served if we fail to warn the world of its sin. If I see someone about to cross a street and he does not notice a car bearing down upon him, my warning is an act of love, not criticism. Our warnings to those about to be destroyed by sin must likewise be acts of love, not anger.

Indeed, we know how greatly the Messiah loved His disciples, yet when He needed to, He did not withhold correction or even, on occasion, rebuke. His words, though, came from the same heart that labored long hours in ministry to the people, healing, delivering, and caring for them. Jesus' reproof was clearly the expression of His love.

HOW CAN WE REVEAL CHRIST?

When Christ evaluated the churches in the book of Revelation, He did not withhold His warnings from them. However, He also presented hope, together with His promises. He communicated encouragement and specifically acknowledged what virtues each had attained. If all we present to sinners are their failings without acknowledging the good graces given to them by God, our correction falls short of the character of Christ.

Thus, the real issue at hand is not how we handle others' sins, but how, in the midst of their sins, we reveal Christ. God is not asking us to be silent in the face of iniquity, but to communicate the full spectrum of Jesus' heart—to appreciate virtue when we see it and to give encouragement where it's needed. The life of a mature Christian can speak the *"truth in love"* (Eph. 4:15) and communicate as much love as truth.

JESUS IS OUR EXAMPLE

Even when people do not repent, we must remain in Christlike intercession for sinners. Jesus did not condemn Jerusalem even as He warned it of coming judgments. He did not just reproach the city for what was wrong; He wept over it.

Christ alone must be our model. We must avoid emulating angry, politically disappointed Christians; our goal is to represent Jesus. Indeed, our openness to the nature of Christ diminishes the longer we harbor unforgiveness or resentment toward sinners. If our hearts become hard, we become hard.

BEWARE OF "COLD LOVE"

It is specifically in this regard that Jesus has a warning for Christians today. While speaking of the conditions in the world at the end of the age, He says, *"Because lawlessness is increased, most people's love will grow cold"* (Matt. 24:12).

I know many Christians who think that this verse is saying that the lawlessness will increase because love has grown cold, but that is not what Jesus was saying. He was saying that, because of the degree and perversity of sin, *the love of many of His followers will grow cold.* The issue is not that the world has cold love, for how could it have anything but cold love? The issue is with God's people who, when they see abounding iniquity, grow angry and cautious; the warning is for saints, not sinners!

It would be a great deception to imagine that any of us is immune to cold love. There are times before Jesus returns when the world will seem utterly out of control. Christians will be wounded, and often enraged, by the degenerating moral conditions around them. It is our love that is in danger.

CHOOSE GRACE OVER ANGER

What is one of the roots of cold love? Often, if we do not go directly to the person who we feel has sinned against us (see Matthew 18:15), anger begins to seethe within us toward him. The word *seethe* originally meant "to soak or saturate in a liquid." In time, it came to mean "to boil." Today, both definitions fit. An unforgiven offense soaks into our thoughts, then steadily rises to a boil in our spirits. We may have suffered genuine injustices; however, seething over them can consume our souls. Whether or not we are able to speak immediately with the person who is in sin, we must always first go to the Lord. The King James Version renders the warning from Matthew 24:12 like this: *"Because iniquity shall abound, the love of many shall wax cold."* Yet, consider also that Paul told us, *"Where sin increased, grace abounded all the more"* (Rom. 5:20). So we have a choice: we can either let our hearts harden with anger or find grace that is greater, more powerful, than sin.

John wrote, *"If anyone sees his brother committing a sin not leading to death, he shall ask and God will for him give life to those who commit sin"* (1 John 5:16). In truth, the very first place we should go when we are offended is to the Lord. It is in Him that we find the correct attitude to respond with grace to the sinner's condition.

Having said that, the best time to talk to people about their sin is *after* God has talked to us about our attitudes. When we speak to them of what we perceive they have done wrong, it must be mercy speaking in humility, not wrath expressed in self-righteousness. Our call in proclaiming the Word of God is to represent Jesus Christ in all things. His nature is the perfect embodiment of both grace and truth.

> *Lord, show me how to be motivated by love, compelled by mercy, and consumed with redemption, even while I speak the truth to the disobedient and sinners. Help me, Lord, to be as concerned about grace as I am about truth, that I might fully reveal Your heart when I speak.*

The Power of One Christlike Life...

Saul of Tarsus
New birth, circa 35 A.D., on the road to Damascus
d. circa 67 A.D., Rome

Saul of Tarsus

Saul's becoming Paul involved more than a name change. Saul was his Hebrew name, but when he became the great Apostle to the Gentiles, Luke called him by his Gentile name, Paul. (See Acts 13:9.)

Paul seems to have come from an influential family and was raised in strict observance of the Hebrew faith, although he was also a Roman citizen. He was present at Stephen's stoning and later sought official approval by the high priest to persecute Christians.

It was while he was on his way to Damascus with that evil intent that he encountered the life-changing presence of Jesus Christ. Temporarily blinded by this encounter, Paul was made to see clearly the reality of the true Messiah. As zealously as he had persecuted Christians, he now became fervent in his passion to take the Gospel to the world. Commissioned by Christ Himself, Paul was committed to the purpose to which he had been called: *"To open their* [the Gentiles'] *eyes, in order to turn them from darkness to light, and from the power of Satan to God, that they may receive forgiveness of sins and an inheritance among those who are sanctified by faith in Me"* (Acts 26:18 NKJV). It is little wonder that Paul's message was one of grace and mercy to all men since he had received both from the One whom he had persecuted.

That the church leaders at first received Paul with suspicion is understandable. That he suffered in his service to Christ is unquestionable. He wrote of being beaten, shipwrecked, imprisoned, and in constant peril, but his greatest burden was for the churches. (See 2 Corinthians 11:24–28.) That he was used mightily by God is indisputable.

Because of his many letters to the churches and his three missionary journeys, Paul helped Christianity grow from a small group of followers to a worldwide faith. Centuries later, Paul's teaching played a powerful role in the Reformation. His influence continues to impact the world as people read and study his New Testament writings. Much of New Testament theology is based on the doctrines inspired by the Holy Spirit and recorded and taught by Paul. His universal message of the Gospel continues to sound throughout history: *"There is neither Jew nor Greek, there is neither slave nor free man, there is neither male nor female; for you are all one in Christ Jesus"* (Gal. 3:28).

Four

From Indignation to Intercession

And when day came, He called His disciples to Him;
and chose twelve of them, whom He also named as
apostles: Simon, whom He also named Peter, and
Andrew his brother; and James and John; and
Philip and Bartholomew; and Matthew and Thomas;
James the son of Alphaeus, and Simon who was
called the Zealot; Judas the son of James, and Judas
Iscariot, who became a traitor.
—Luke 6:13–16

J udas Iscariot had traveled both with Jesus and
His disciples. Along with the others, he had been
used mightily to *"heal the sick, raise the dead,*
cleanse the lepers, [and] *cast out demons"* (Matt.
10:8). Numbered among the original twelve, Judas
knew the excitement, joy, and power of walking with
Jesus.

Yet Judas had a serious character flaw, a moral
weakness. Scripture reveals that, despite the fact
that God was using him, Judas *"was a thief, and as*
he had the money box, he used to pilfer what was put
into it" (John 12:6).

It is significant, my friend, that Jesus allowed a thief to carry the money box. Sometimes we think the Lord is going to challenge us on every issue, but there are times when His silence about our repeated sin is His rebuke. Judas knew that what he was doing was wrong, but since Jesus didn't directly confront him, he minimized the severity of his iniquity. Perhaps he rationalized that, if pilfering were truly bad, God would not still use him to work miracles.

How a little leaven leavens the whole lump! A relatively minor sin left unattended can lead to a major sin that destroys our lives. Judas *"became a traitor."* He started out in ministry loyal to Jesus, but then began lying about the finances until his deceitful exterior completely hid a very corrupt interior. Judas was a thief who became a traitor, eventually taking his own life. His unrepentant compromise went from bad to worse, and it destroyed him.

IS ANGER JUSTIFIABLE?

In a similar way, unrepented and unresolved sin can change us from committed disciples of Christ to those who disown His mission. Today, Christians look at the world and see injustice, immorality, and corruption. The anger we feel because of these things is not only understandable, it seems justified. Why shouldn't we be angry at what we see? Indeed, in many instances we are actually watching hell manifest itself through people and situations in the world!

Knowing we would grieve over the evil in the world, God's Word tells us, *"BE ANGRY, AND yet DO NOT SIN"* (Eph. 4:26). We must discern at what point anger festers into sin. The verse continues, *"Do not let the sun go down on your anger"* (v. 26).

We can be legitimately angry about things that are truly wrong, but by sundown our indignation must find a more noble, redemptive attitude of expression. We must reach for forgiveness, intercessory prayer, and a love that *"covers a multitude of sins"* (1 Pet. 4:8). Otherwise, Paul warned, we will *"give the devil an opportunity"* (Eph. 4:27).

What happens when we do not allow the Holy Spirit to transform our frustrations? Self-righteousness begins to manifest in our souls. We become embittered, judgmental, and cynical. A cynic is one who is "a habitual doubter." Do you know any Christians who are cynical?

The worst thing that happens when we turn angry and cease praying is that we, like Judas, betray Christ. How? When we disown Christ's mission of intercession, redemption, and forgiveness, we turn our backs on sinners destined for hell.

Judas changed from an apostle into a person he never intended to become: he *became* a traitor. Our anger, left unattended, will do the same to us. It causes us to degenerate into something we never planned on becoming: "Christian Pharisees." By allowing self-righteousness and a judgmental spirit to grow in the soil of unrepentant anger, we become worse in God's eyes than the evil that offended us.

Today's church is overstocked with angry Christians. What can we do? We must turn indignation into intercession. We must make our heartache work for us, aligning ourselves with Christ in the prayer of redemption. Otherwise, we betray Christ's purpose with our anger.

"IT'S THE PRINCIPLE"

I know Christians who refuse to surrender their anger to God in many different situations. These are people who love their country, possess high morals, and seek to walk in integrity, yet they feel perfectly justified in being embittered about certain situations! Under the guise, "It's the principle of the thing," they are completely unalarmed by their un-Christlike attitudes.

Where in the Bible does God permit Christians to harbor hatred and an unforgiving attitude toward anyone? When was it that God gave permission to Jesus' followers to remain angry toward a person for months, or even years?

Thank God, Jesus didn't look down from the cross at the Pharisees and say, "You need to be taught a lesson. I love you, but it's the principle." No. He prayed, *"Father, forgive them"* (Luke 23:34). Then, amazingly, He covered their sin, saying, *"They do not know what they are doing"* (v. 34).

ANGER IS NO LITTLE SIN

The sense of Christian indignation infiltrating the church has not come from heaven. James clearly tells us that the *"anger of man does not achieve the righteousness of God"* (James 1:20). Don't dismiss your anger as a little sin; it disqualified Moses from entering the Promised Land!

It's time to deal with our indignation and lack of forgiveness. It is a terrible witness to the non-Christian world. You see, even though the unsaved don't know much about the Scriptures, they still possess a God-given sense of who Christ is when it comes to real-life issues. Before they will join a church, they will watch how Christians deal with imperfect people.

Things bigger than our indignation about right and wrong are at stake. The world is watching how we relate to those who are morally wrong, even when we are biblically right. And it is watching to see if we look and sound like the Savior or like the Pharisees.

But more crucial than how the world sees us is how Christ sees us. He is watching what is happening to our hearts. He asks each of us a simple question: Do you know what you're becoming? Are you turning your indignation into intercession?

Lord Jesus, help me! When did I switch from loving to judging? When did I replace the glow, the smile of Your love, with this unceasing, angry frown? Master, like Judas, I have become what I never set out to be: a traitor to Your redemptive purpose. Forgive me. Cleanse me of my anger and pride. Restore my heart until I love as You have loved me, until I stand for others in their need as You have stood for me in mine. For Your glory. Amen.

The Power of One Christlike Life...

Brother Lawrence of the Resurrection
b. 1611, Herimenil, France
d. February 12, 1691, Paris, France

Brother Lawrence of the Resurrection

*A*lthough he lived in relative obscurity as a lay brother in a Parisian monastery among Discalced (barefoot) Carmelites, Nicholas Herman, given the name Lawrence of the Resurrection, exemplified the power of one Christlike life. When Brother Lawrence died, Abbé Joseph de Beaufort gave his eulogy, which Beaufort later published, along with letters and remembrances of conversations that he had had with his friend. That book, *The Practice of the Presence of God,* was first published in 1692, yet it continues to be read today. Its simple but powerful message has inspired readers to follow the example of one who lived in constant communion with his Lord. Brother Lawrence said that he came to a state where it was as difficult "not to think of God" as it had been "to accustom [himself] to thinking of Him at the beginning."

Brother Lawrence was converted at age eighteen when he saw a barren tree in winter. Realizing that with spring's return, the tree would again flower and bear fruit, he sensed the awesome "providence and power of God." His love for God caused him to give himself in complete abandonment to Him.

For years he served in the kitchen of the monastery, an assignment not of his preference. Yet, with the implicit trust of a child asking his father for help, Brother Lawrence asked God for the grace to remain in Him as he worked; he prayed to be able to keep God company as he fulfilled his duties. Although his formal education was limited, he listened and learned from the Great Teacher. After conversing with Brother Lawrence, a bishop said that the "greatness and purity of his love for God made him live, even while on earth, like those who enjoy God's presence in heaven."

Brother Lawrence believed in a living, active faith. Rather than relying on inconstant emotions, he urged others to "remain faithful in the dry periods." He knew that he could approach God at all times, "without fear of being an annoyance," and he came to God out of love, rather than out of a desire for His gifts.

As his fellow monks were drawn to him because of his spiritual maturity, inner peace, joy, and practical teachings, so have countless other Christians benefited from following Brother Lawrence's practice of constant devotion and awareness of the presence of God.

Five

One Man

A familiar statement in American Christianity and a popular quote that has been prevalent for the last few years is, "If God doesn't destroy America, He will have to apologize to Sodom and Gomorrah." I have heard this comment repeated in churches and revival meetings; it was actually quoted by secular newspapers, epitomizing the Christian perspective expounded at political conventions.

For most, this remark is simply a clever or emphatic way of saying that America needs to repent, and that, as a nation, Americans are in danger of invoking God's wrath. Within this rhetorical sphere, the expression certainly has its value, and a number of Christians have repeated it with this intent. In fact, for a while I used it myself in this rhetorical sense.

But the Holy Spirit began to check me about repeating this view of America. First, because it isn't really true (a majority of Americans are not violent homosexuals); second, because God has been doing something wonderful in our land, uniting Christians and raising up an ever resurgent prayer movement that is integral to the divine plan. We are moving in a direction different from wrath, which the Lord not only recognizes, but also has inspired.

Yet, when I questioned a number of church leaders about this "God-about-to-destroy-America" attitude, I was amazed to discover that a majority actually believed this statement not to be rhetorical, but true. In their eyes, America was worse than Sodom and Gomorrah. As I probed, I uncovered a deep bitterness in a number of leaders toward the United States. In fact, because I did not share the deep-seated bitterness of one colleague toward the United States, I was questioned as to whether I had compromised my stand on holiness!

The true measure of spirituality is not how angry we become toward sinners, but how Christlike; our mission is not to see men destroyed, but redeemed.

For the sake of illustration, let's assume my colleague's view is correct, that this nation is as evil as Sodom. In the historical account, Sodom and Gomorrah present the pattern of wickedness, but let's also examine the pattern of righteousness in the story. Let's look at how Abraham responded to God's warning of imminent destruction.

GOD'S RESPONSE TO MERCIFUL INTERCESSION

When Abraham was confronted with the possibility of Sodom's destruction, he did not immediately jump on the "Destroy Sodom" bandwagon; instead, he went before the Lord and prayed for mercy for the city. Abraham's prayer is an amazing study on the effect a mercy-motivated intercessor has on the heart of God. My objective here is to look past this event and gaze into the heart of God, which is revealed in the discourse between the Lord and Abraham.

As we look at Abraham's prayer, we discover the key, the power we have in intercession. We discover the element the Lord is seeking in providing us the privilege of prayer. And what is that? He is looking for a spark of hope within us, for us to recognize a mercy-reason that would justify delaying or canceling wrath. We must not belittle this principle, for in it is great hope for our land as well.

Let us consider also the Lord's initial response to Sodom's sin. First, He revealed to Abraham, His servant, what He was about to do. Why? *Because God desired Abraham to intercede.* When the Lord informed His servant of what was wrong in the world, it was not so that Abraham could simply criticize it, but so that he would intercede for mercy. Remember, God delights in mercy (Mic. 7:18) and takes *"no pleasure in the death of the wicked"* (Ezek. 33:11). The Lord always seeks opportunities of mercy. Therefore, let's take note of how Abraham approached the Almighty:

> *Then the men turned away from there and went toward Sodom, while Abraham was still standing before the LORD. And Abraham came near and said, "Wilt Thou indeed sweep away the righteous with the wicked? Suppose there are fifty righteous within the*

city; wilt Thou indeed sweep it away and not spare the place for the sake of the fifty righteous who are in it? Far be it from Thee to do such a thing, to slay the righteous with the wicked, so that the righteous and the wicked are treated alike. Far be it from Thee! Shall not the Judge of all the earth deal justly?"

(Gen. 18:22–25)

NO COMPROMISE WITH SIN

Notice, Abraham did not pray from a place of anger. He never said, "God, it's about time You killed the perverts." There was no finger-pointing vindictiveness in Abraham's soul. Somehow, we have come to believe that non-compromising Christians must also be angry. Abraham never compromised with Sodom's depraved culture, yet he was above fleshly reaction. In fact, throughout his prayer, Abraham never mentioned what was wrong in Sodom. He appealed, instead, to the mercy and integrity of the Lord.

This is vitally important for us, because Jesus said, *"If you are Abraham's children, do the deeds of Abraham"* (John 8:39). One of Abraham's most noteworthy deeds involved his intercessory prayer for Sodom, the most perverse city in the world!

Abraham first acknowledged the Lord's integrity, then he spoke to the Lord's mercy. *"Suppose there are fifty righteous within the city; wilt Thou indeed sweep it away and not spare the place for the sake of the fifty?"* (Gen. 18:24).

The Lord knew that it would be unjust to slay the righteous with the wicked; Abraham's prayer did not enlighten the Lord of some unknown fact. But the nature of life on earth is this: God works with man to establish the future and, in the process of determining reality, He always prepares a merciful alternative. In other words, urgent, redemptive prayer shoots straight through the mercy door and enters God's heart. This door is never shut, especially since we have a High Priest, Jesus Christ, ministering at the mercy seat in the heavens (Heb. 8:1). It is open each and every time we pray. Listen to how the Lord answered Abraham's prayer for mercy: *"If I find in Sodom fifty righteous within the city, then I will spare the whole place on their account"* (Gen. 18:26).

How the truth of God's mercy flies in the face of those so eager to judge their nation! Incredibly, the Lord said He would spare the whole of Sodom if He found fifty righteous people there. Now, keep this in mind: the Hebrew word for *"spare"* means more than "not destroy"; it also means "to forgive or pardon." This is a tremendous revelation about the living God. He will minimize, delay, or even cancel a day of reckoning as long as Christ-inspired prayer is being offered for sinners!

GOD'S ABUNDANT LOVE

Time and again throughout the Scriptures the Lord proclaims an ever present truth about His nature: He is *"slow to anger, and abounding in loving-kindness"* (Exod. 34:6). Do we believe this? Here it

63

is, demonstrated right before our eyes in the Scriptures. He tells us plainly that a few righteous people in a city can preserve that area from divine wrath.

Abraham knew the love of God. He was an intimate friend of God's. Abraham, in truth, had a clear view into the heart of God based on his own experiences. This interceding patriarch had seen the Almighty bless, prosper, and forgive him, so he pressed God's mercy toward its limits.

"What if there are forty?"

The Lord would spare it for forty.

Abraham bargained, "Thirty?"

He would spare it for thirty.

"Twenty?"

He finally secured the Lord's promise not to destroy the city if He could find just ten righteous people there. On God's scales, wrath is on one side and mercy on the other. Put the entire city of Sodom with all its sin and perversion on one side. The scales tip toward wrath as the weightiness of advanced wickedness runs rampant through an entire city. Let's assume that there were two hundred thousand evil people in Sodom. It is weighed heavily on the side of evil. Yet, on the other side, place just ten righteous individuals. As the ten are placed on the scale, the spiritual weight of the righteous, with just ten, tips the scales toward mercy.

In God's heart, the substance of the righteous far outweighs the wickedness of the evil! Herein we discover what we are seeking in the heart of God through prayer: the Lord would spare (forgive) sinful Sodom, with its gangs of violent homosexuals, because of the influence of ten godly people who dwelt within it!

How about Your Community?

Now, let's think of your city: are there ten good people among you? Consider your region. Do you think there might be one hundred praying people living within its borders, people who are pleading with God for mercy? What about nationwide? Do you suppose there might be ten thousand people interceding for your country? God said He would spare Sodom for ten righteous people. Do you think God would spare your nation for ten thousand righteous?

I live in a metropolitan area in the United States that has about two hundred thousand people. I can list by name scores of righteous individuals, including pastors, intercessors, youth workers, black folks, white folks, Hispanic folks, native Americans, Asian Americans, Christian business people, moms, dads, godly teenagers, praying grandmothers, secretaries, policemen, and on and on who live here—far more than the ten righteous needed to save a place like Sodom. There are many here who care about this city.

Think about your church and the greater church community in your city. Aren't there at least ten honorable people who sincerely care about your community, who desire that God would bring revival? Remember, the Lord said He would spare Sodom for the sake of the ten.

God's Love for the Righteous

One last thought concerning Abraham and Sodom: when the Lord's messengers came to rescue

Lot and his family, Lot hesitated. Pressured by two of God's avenging angels to flee to the mountains, Lot asked that he and his family might instead escape to Zoar. As one of the angels granted his request, God's messenger uttered something amazing. The angel said, *"Hurry, escape there, for I cannot do anything until you arrive there"* (Gen. 19:22).

"I cannot do anything." Think about this, my friends: God had put a limitation on His wrath! As long as the righteous dwelt in the city, it was protected. Indeed, when Lot fled to Zoar, though fire and brimstone fell and consumed every inhabitant of every community in the valley, Zoar was protected without a single casualty. Why? Because the righteous were there.

JUST ONE

Abraham stopped his prayer at ten people. But I will tell you something that is most profound: man of faith that he was, Abraham stopped praying too soon. The Lord reveals in Scripture that His mercy will extend even further. The scene is sinful Jerusalem. Yet, listen to what the Almighty told Jeremiah:

> *Roam to and fro through the streets of Jerusalem, and look now, and take note. And seek in her open squares, if you can find a man, if there is one who does justice, who seeks truth, then I will pardon her.* (Jer. 5:1)

He says, *"If you can find a man...who does justice,...then I will pardon [Jerusalem]."* One holy

66

person in an unholy city can actually turn away God's wrath. One godly individual who remains righteous while living among the ungodly, who cares for a community or a family or a school or a neighborhood or a church, swings open the door for mercy.

My friends, it is not a little thing to God that He has a soul that remains righteous in an unrighteous world. If just one heart refuses to give in to the intimidation of increasing wickedness, if that one refuses to submit to hopelessness, fear, or unbelief, it is enough to exact from heaven a delay of wrath. You, my friend, can be that one who obtains forgiveness for your city, who stands between the godless past and a God-filled future!

Mercy far outweighs wrath. Mercy always triumphs over judgment. You see, whenever a person operates in intercessory mercy, the tender passions of Christ are unveiled in the world. Do you truly want to know who Jesus is? Consider this: He ever lives to make intercession (Heb. 7:25); He is seated at the right hand of God the Father, praying on our behalf (Rom. 8:34). He is not waiting in heaven, eagerly desiring an opportunity to destroy the world. He is praying for mercy. This is His nature.

Christ, the second person of the Trinity, is God in His mercy form. He is God, loving the world, dying for its sins, and paying the price of redemption. Christ is the mercy of God satisfying the justice of God.

God declared that man was to be made in the divine image, and it is this image of Christ the Redeemer that reveals our pattern. We are to follow the mercy path set by Christ. The Scriptures boldly declare God's goal for the church: *"As He is, so also are we in this world"* (1 John 4:17).

Thus, the nature of Christ is manifest in our world every time redemptive intercession is offered to God for sinners. Jesus came to earth to fulfill the mercy of God. His title is Redeemer. His role is Savior. He is the Good Shepherd who *"lays down His life for* [His] *sheep"* (John 10:11). God calls us to be like Jesus who, in turn, says to us, *"As the Father has sent Me, I also send you"* (John 20:21). We are sent by Jesus with the purpose of redemption.

The manifestation on earth of one Christlike intercessor perfectly restrains God's need for judgment on a society. Let me say it again: *"Mercy triumphs over judgment"* (James 2:13). Mercy corresponds exactly with God's heart. Yes, it is true. One man or woman who reveals Christ's heart on earth will defer God's judgment from heaven.

> *Lord Jesus, forgive me for devaluing the power of prayer. Forgive me for underestimating how passionately You desire to reveal Your mercy. Lord, give me grace to be one who never ceases to cry out to You for mercy. Lord, let me not base my obedience on what my eyes see or my ears hear, but upon the revelation of Your mercy; let me build my life on Thee. Amen!*

The Power of One Christlike Life...

General William Booth
b. April 10, 1829, Nottingham, Nottinghamshire, England
d. August 20, 1912, London, England

General William Booth

Known as the father and mother of the Salvation Army, William and Catherine Booth were joined together in heart and in calling. Both students of the writings of John Wesley, they embraced the experience of sanctification and recognized it as a "glorious reality."

William was converted in a Wesleyan church and became a Methodist New Connexion minister. Before long, though, his call to evangelism was stronger than the church officials' directive for him to stay at his appointed circuit. One day, as he looked out on his large congregation, he was driven to resign, asking himself, "Why am I here, with this crowded chapel of people who *want* to hear the message? Why am I not outside, bringing the message of God to those who don't want it?" His passion for the lost punctuated the charge he would later give to those in the Salvation Army, "Go for souls, and go for the worst."

Booth's open-air preaching among the poor in the East end of London eventually led to the formation of the Christian Mission. At first, those who joined with Booth were called "A Volunteer Army" and were organized in a military fashion. Later, Booth would strike the word *volunteer* and replace it with *salvation,* bringing the focus of their mission to their name.

The musical bands, now an integral part of the movement, were started almost by accident. A man in Salisbury offered the services of himself and his sons to act as bodyguards to protect the Salvationists during their street meetings. He brought along their instruments to accompany the singing, and the first Salvation Army band was born.

One would think that the churches and government officials alike would have embraced the humanitarian and spiritual services of the Salvation Army. On the contrary, members of the corps were beaten, jailed, spat open, and even murdered. Booth was branded by some as the Antichrist. Moreover, what was known as a Skeleton Army, supported largely by brewers and ruffians, persecuted the Salvationists while the police deliberately turned their heads.

Some hated Booth's methods, judging his street corner services as irreverent and indecent. Many were appalled at what they considered to be his improper elevation of women. It was his wife Catherine who had changed his mind. He came to recognize the abilities of women to preach and to reach the lost. At one point, he remarked, "My best men are women!"

Others disagreed with his abandonment of baptism and the sacraments. Booth felt that those who had been rescued from sin's depths needed to be totally dependent upon God and not on ritual. He was especially concerned that recovering alcoholics would not slip back into their addiction from tasting the Communion wine.

However, even its objectors had to admire the Salvation Army's results. The slogan "Soup, Soap, and Salvation!" encapsulated the Army's philosophy. Booth and his soldiers were concerned not only with the spiritual condition of people but also with their social welfare. His controversial book *In Darkest England and the Way Out* became an overnight best-seller. His proposed social changes included plans for an employment office, a bank to give small loans so that workers could purchase tools, a farm where the unemployed could be trained, a bureau where his officers would assist in locating missing persons, inexpensive lodging where men could find a decent and safe place to stay, a legal aid system for the poor, and an emigration strategy that would relocate people in order to give them a new start. Although some judged his ideas to be impractical, others supported his plans. The efforts of the Salvationists produced results that turned persecution into hard-won respect.

It was through Booth's activism that match factories in England stopped using yellow phosphorus, which poisoned their workers, and switched to harmless red phosphorus. Salvationists were responsible for starting a work among the lepers in Java, transforming the criminal tribes of India into law-abiding citizens, and closing the doors of the infamous penal colony on Devil's Island. The first disaster relief fund was started by the Army as a result of the San Francisco earthquake in April 1906. Over 16,000 homeless people were cared for in a camp set up in nearby Beulah Park. Today the Army is noted for its continuing response to human needs—both spiritual and physical.

Three months before his death, General Booth proclaimed, "While there yet remains one dark soul without the light of God, I'll fight—I'll fight to the very end." The Salvation Army continues to fight for the salvation of the lost and the betterment of the poor and outcast.

Six

Prayer Changes the Mind of God

In the last chapter we observed the effect mercy has on the heart of God: the Lord would have spared Sodom for the sake of ten righteous souls. Then, to our amazement, we discovered that God's mercy would have gone still further. Even as the Almighty's wrath was about to fall on Jerusalem, the Lord said that if there had been just one man of integrity in the city, that man's presence could have gained pardon for the entire city.

CHRIST IN YOU

The Lord's willingness to extend mercy has not always been understood by the church. We must rediscover true, biblical Christianity. We have been content to possess a religion focused on what Jesus did without actually manifesting the reality of who Jesus is. Truly, our destiny does not find sure footing until the actual life of Christ emerges in redemption through us.

This Christlike transformation of the church was of the utmost concern for Paul. *"My children,"* he wrote, *"with whom I am again in labor until*

Christ is formed in you" (Gal. 4:19). Christianity is nothing less than Christ Himself entering our lives and conforming them to His likeness.

Again, Paul wrote, this time to the Corinthians, *"For we who live are constantly being delivered over to death for Jesus' sake, that the life of Jesus also may be manifested in our mortal flesh"* (2 Cor. 4:11).

Do we see this truth? Basic Christianity is the *"life of Jesus...manifested in our mortal flesh."* But what does this mean? It means that the purpose of redemption, as revealed in Jesus' life, is revealed again through us. Anything less than Jesus' very life revealed through us will never be more than religion, nor will it satisfy our thirst to know the substance of God.

You see, when we accept Christ into our lives, it means not only that at death we gain passage to heaven, but also that in life Jesus gains passage to earth. Our salvation gives Jesus flesh and blood access to again bring mercy to the specific needs of our world.

Paul said he was in spiritual travail, suffering the pains of birth, to see the actual, substantial life of Christ functioning in the church. What is this life of Christ? It is love made perfect in an imperfect world.

To the church in Philippi, Paul explained Christ's life this way:

> *Have this attitude in yourselves which was also in Christ Jesus, who, although He existed in the form of God, did not regard equality with God a thing to be grasped, but*

emptied Himself, taking the form of a bond-servant, and being made in the likeness of men. And being found in appearance as a man, He humbled Himself by becoming obedient to the point of death, even death on a cross.   (Phil. 2:5–8)

To have Christ's attitude in ourselves is to possess the motive of the Redeemer of the world; it is to be infused with the compassion of the One who prayed for those who crucified Him, *"Father, forgive them"* (Luke 23:34). Such characteristics are simply unfamiliar to us. To attain Christ's mind, God calls us to a realignment of our thoughts, attitudes, and motives until we think and act in perfect synchrony with Christ's nature. We will not arrive at this overnight; it is a lifetime pursuit. Still, it means we must set our goal not to be judgmental but redemptive in our motives.

We have been granted access to, or possession of, the very mind of Christ (1 Cor. 2:16)! To think as Christ Himself is not merely a doctrinally based mind-set or a religious outlook, but a perspective shaped by a motive to bring redemption. If you truly desire Christlikeness, you will measure yourself by how aggressively you work to see mercy triumph over judgment.

From His eternal vantage point of *"equality with God"* (Phil. 2:6), Christ saw the world in all its sinfulness. Knowing the very worst of man's blood lust and immorality, He could have simply allowed divine wrath to fall. Yet He beheld the extremes of the world's evil, from the long Dark Ages to the carnage of war throughout the ages. He saw the child exploitation and abuse; He knew of the age of abortion and genocide. He was fully conscious of the electronic age and how Satan would manipulate the entertainment industry to exploit man's fallen nature. Having seen the vile corruption that infects the world, instead of condemning the world, amazingly, He died for it.

"Let this mind be in you, which was also in Christ Jesus" (Phil. 2:5 KJV). This is the new paradigm: our perception of the world must conform to what perfect love would do in all things.

INTERCESSION: THE ESSENCE OF CHRIST

Throughout the ages, the Son of God has sought to reveal Himself through the intercession of the saints. The mercy prayer triumphed, whether He inspired people to follow His example of compassion in Old or New Testament times. When judgment for sin was imminent, and Christ was revealed through redemptive intercession, divine wrath was restrained, delayed, or even averted. Israel often became wanton. However, when mercy pled for time, though iniquity still abounded, grace abounded even more (Rom. 5:20).

What flashes forth in brilliant moments of redemption in Old Testament examples is raised to full stature in the glory of Christ. Indeed, since His first coming, Christ has purposed to raise up an army of Spirit-filled individuals whose prayers and actions multiply mercy opportunities for the Father. Yet even before Christ's incarnation, the pattern of God's redemptive power produced many righteous saints whose prayers turned the heart of God from judgment to mercy. One such individual was Moses.

THE LIFE OF AN INTERCESSOR

Moses exemplifies a man growing through the stages of intercession. Although he was born an Israelite, as an infant he was taken by Pharaoh's daughter and raised as an Egyptian. During his first forty years, Moses was *"educated in all the learning of the Egyptians,"* and he became *"a man of power in words and deeds"* (Acts 7:22).

As he matured, however, a time came when he could no longer remain detached from the sufferings of his Israelite brethren; he began to identify with the people of God. Here is how the book of Hebrews renders this transition in Moses' life:

> *By faith Moses, when he had grown up, refused to be called the son of Pharaoh's daughter; choosing rather to endure illtreatment with the people of God, than to enjoy the passing pleasures of sin.*
>
> (Heb. 11:24–25)

The Scriptures explain that when we leave our places of privilege and number ourselves with others in need, we are, in some fashion, revealing the nature of Christ. (See Isaiah 53.) Hebrews 11:26 confirms this point, for it says that Moses considered *"the reproach of Christ greater riches than the treasures of Egypt."* When Moses chose to *"endure illtreatment with the people of God"* (v. 25), he was, in fact, bearing *"the reproach of Christ"* (v. 26).

77

Christ is God. He is the fullness of the Godhead in bodily form and, thus, beyond reproach. However, the reproach Christ bore came from His identification with sinners. The Pharisees reproached Christ because He accepted the ungodly into His company. Moses, a prince in Egypt, united himself with the humiliation and dehumanization of his brethren, who were slaves in Egypt. Yet, in so doing, he discovered the nature of Christ, considering the *"reproach of Christ"* to be actually *"greater riches than the treasures of Egypt"* (v. 26).

The quickening in Moses was actually a Christ-awakening. However, though Moses was awakened spiritually, he had not yet been trained. He was still immature and unfamiliar with the ways of God. His heart was open to Christ, but his mind was still in control of his own decisions; in presumption, he struck and killed an Egyptian. The Lord will not reject us for our fleshly beginnings, but neither will He endorse them. They invariably fail to bring deliverance.

We know the story well. Moses fled and spent the next forty years in the wilderness. Alone with God, his pride and self-will were broken. Indeed, without brokenness, no one can serve the Lord. Brokenness is openness to God. When the Lord finally sent Moses back to Egypt, he went with true power as God's anointed leader of Israel, and he went as Israel's chief intercessor.

What is a spiritual leader? He is one who is given the task of revealing God's promise to an imperfect people, and then he remains committed in prayer for that people until God's promise comes to pass. This is the nature of true intercession. Though we may indeed hate the sin that holds people in bondage, we cannot despise people for their rebellion and unbelief; this is the very reason they need our prayers!

Throughout Israel's long wilderness journey, Moses positioned himself between the imminent judgment of God and the available, but inactivated, mercy of God. Time and again, he secured forgiveness from the Almighty, which allowed the people of Israel, even in their imperfections, to move forward. Throughout their entire forty-year journey, Moses stayed before God, never abandoning his role as intercessor, never doubting God's willingness to forgive the people.

Remember, a leader's task is to bring an imperfect people from promise to fulfillment. Moses fulfilled his task, though he himself was neither perfect nor immune to his own fleshly reactions. Frequently, he had to deal with Israel's criticism of himself and Aaron. Often, the Israelites fell into unbelief, murmuring and complaining against him, and he grew angry. Yet he never failed to deal with his attitude and return to prayer for Israel.

At the same time, Moses himself was learning God's ways. An important lesson came when Amalek rose up to war against Israel.

> *Moses said to Joshua, "Choose men for us, and go out, fight against Amalek. Tomorrow I will station myself on the top of the hill with the staff of God in my hand." And Joshua did as Moses told him, and fought*

against Amalek; and Moses, Aaron, and Hur went up to the top of the hill. So it came about when Moses held his hand up, that Israel prevailed, and when he let his hand down, Amalek prevailed. But Moses' hands were heavy. Then they took a stone and put it under him, and he sat on it; and Aaron and Hur supported his hands, one on one side and one on the other. Thus his hands were steady until the sun set. So Joshua overwhelmed Amalek and his people with the edge of the sword. (Exod. 17:9–13)

Moses realized that Israel's victory was attached to his posture before God. For leaders and intercessors, the victory that God's people are reaching for is often, in some measure, attached to their stance before God. The position of leaders in the "prayer posture" will add power and victory to the people in the "fight posture."

There are marriages in your neighborhood that are going to have a breakthrough because you stand before God with your hands lifted in prayer. There are breakthroughs in schools that will come, not because anyone is doing anything differently, but because you have placed yourself before God and are in prayer. Communities will have greater peace as criminals with uplifted hands surrender to authorities because intercessors, with uplifted hands, surrender to God in prayer. The person who stands before God and prays is valuable to God and instrumental in gaining the victory.

INTERCESSION AND DIVINE PROTECTION

Years ago I pastored a small church. Almost without fail, each night I would pray for the congregation before I went to sleep. One night, however, I simply forgot to pray. At seven-thirty the next morning, I received a call. One of the men in the church had been in a serious accident. Immediately the thought entered my mind, "I did not pray last night," but then I dismissed it. I did not want to accept that my lack of prayer could in any way have contributed to what happened.

About six months later, again I went to sleep without praying for the church. The next morning I woke to a distressing phone call. One of the farmers in the church had been harvesting when both his feet were caught and mangled in a jammed auger. I thought, "I didn't pray last night," but once more I did not want to accept that people's lives could be left vulnerable by my lack of prayer. Still, the fear of God was on me because of these two accidents, so I made a more committed effort to intercede for my congregation nightly.

The following summer I spoke at a Christian camp and brought my family with me. My youngest son asked me to lie down with him that night. Exhausted, I lay down next to him, and instantly we both fell asleep. When I came home from the camp, I had another phone call waiting. A young woman in the church had rolled her car and crashed into a ditch. Three times in two years I had failed to pray, and each time there was an accident—the only accidents the church experienced. I knew the Lord was revealing to me something that I could no longer resist accepting: *my lack of prayer left people vulnerable to the Enemy.*

Although all three of these people recovered from their injuries, I have never recovered from not praying at night. In addition, I often find myself waking in the middle of the night, interceding for various individuals or situations.

Leaders and intercessors, God gives us spiritual authority to protect those whom we love. As wide as our range of love is, to that degree we have authority in prayer. Such is the unique place we have: whether we are praying for our families, churches, cities, or nations, people will receive certain victories and protection that they otherwise would not have.

Let me share another example of the power of intercession to protect people. Several years ago, for a period of two weeks, a group of local pastors, of which I was a part, gathered each weekday at noon for prayer. We were specifically praying for our city and our mayor. During this time our mayor and his wife came to Christ, and each made a radical commitment to serve Him. However, within the next four months, the Enemy challenged the direction God was taking the city, and our community experienced three murders. The mayor and a couple of pastors consulted together and decided to meet in his office for prayer every Wednesday morning at six o'clock. This prayer continued until his term was up (he chose not to run again). But throughout that time, and for a year and a half afterward, there was not another murder in the city—a total of more than thirty months! When leaders and intercessors pray, God protects.

DON'T LEAVE GOD ALONE!

Returning to our study of Moses, let's look at another time in which Israel sinned. This new scene opens on Mount Sinai where the visible glory of God has descended; in glowing splendor, the Almighty manifests His holiness to three million Israelites. Out of this living fire, the voice of God speaks, and waves of quaking fear roll through the Israelites encamped at the mountain base. In response, Israel's leaders beg Moses that no further words be spoken to them from God. Moses agrees, and he ascends to the mountaintop and enters this frightening holy blaze, remaining there for forty days. (See Exodus 19:17–20:19; 24:18.)

When Moses delayed his return, the Hebrews gathered together their gold and cast for themselves an idol, a golden calf, similar to the idols the Egyptians had worshiped. Be mindful that they did all of this in full view of the glory of God, defying His glory with their idolatry. (See Exodus 31:1–8.)

Nothing angers God more than idolatry, and this brazen act was enough to have destroyed all Israel, both the sinners and those who tolerated their sin in the camp. In response, the Lord said to Moses,

> *I have seen this people, and behold, they are an obstinate people. Now then let Me alone, that My anger may burn against them, and that I may destroy them; and I will make of you a great nation.* (Exod. 32:9–10)

This is an amazing verse. The Lord says, *"Let Me alone."* In the consciousness of the Almighty, judgment cannot come as long as the leader/intercessor does not withdraw his entreaty. In other words, as long as Moses did not let God alone, the Lord would not destroy Israel. Listen to God's words to Moses, *"Let Me alone."*

The goal of an intercessor is to not let God alone. The goal of the Devil is to create just the opposite relationship between you and God. He seeks to separate, or to discourage you from standing before God for your family, your city, your church, or your school. If the Lord has no intercessor, His wrath may potentially be kindled.

"Let Me alone," the Lord said, yet Moses refused. He was compelled by God's very mercy to disobey. This is the only time our direct disobedience brings pleasure to the Lord. Moses refused to leave the ear and heart of God. Why? Because if there is one man standing *"in the gap"* (Ezek. 22:30), God's mercy stays kindled.

Moses became a mature intercessor. He stayed close to God, prevailing in prayer. Even though the Lord said He would make of Moses a great nation, Moses ignored the prospect. He knew that no matter what people he must lead, there would be problems, sin, and failure. No, Moses had come too far to start over. And then he reminded the Lord of the promise He had made to Abraham, Isaac, and Jacob. This journey was about a covenant that was made with Israel's forefathers.

Remember, the assignment is to bring an imperfect people with a promise from God into fulfillment. The intercessor's role is to pray from the beginning of that journey, through the valleys of sin and setbacks, and continue praying until the promise from God is obtained.

You may be a pastor of a church or an intercessor or a parent. Nevertheless, whatever you are praying for, you must have this attitude: "Lord, I am not letting You alone concerning this people." Never pray for judgment or wrath; always pray for mercy. Agree with God that wrath is justified because of man's sin, yet plead with God for mercy to come. Such is the heart that brings heaven to earth and fulfillment to promises. Read in awe the result of Moses' intercession: *"So the LORD changed His mind about the harm which He said He would do to His people"* (Exod. 32:14).

May this be a revelation to us all! *Moses' prayer changed God's mind!* You may have a rebellious child or a mean-spirited boss or someone in your neighborhood who is pushing everyone to the limit. Instinctively, we desire that God would punish the individuals who have wronged us. It is at such a time that we must refuse to take our battles personally. Publicly, Moses was very upset with Israel; privately, he pleaded with God for mercy, and his prayer changed God's mind.

Many people try to predict either the day of Christ's return or the time when judgment will begin in the world. However, in the preceding illustration, we behold another reason why Jesus said no one knows the day or the hour of His return (Matt. 24:36): *prayer changes the mind of God.* In fact, Jesus told us regarding tribulation to *"pray that your flight may not be in the winter"* (v. 20). We minimize its impact, but prayer actually can influence the season when the Great Tribulation will begin.

Much of how God relates to a nation, city, church, or group is based upon how the people in that society pray. The future of a society belongs to those who pray. Prayer, or lack of prayer, sits at the table in the counsel of God's will. Thus, Jesus tells His disciples that whatever two of them agree on *"about anything that they may ask"* (Matt. 18:19), it will be granted by the heavenly Father. Two or three servants of God who refuse to abandon their faithfulness in prayer release the mercy of God directly into the path of those for whom they pray.

For Moses and the Israelites, the outcome was profound: *"So the LORD changed His mind about the harm which He said He would do to His people"* (Exod. 32:14). Think of it: prayer changed God's mind.

> *Lord, thank You for always remaining open to our cries. Help me to persevere, to give You no rest, until You fulfill Your highest purposes with my nation. Thank You that one voice is not too feeble that You cannot hear it, but that You will respond even to one intercessor who stands with You for the cause of mercy.*

The Power of One Christlike Life...

George Müller
b. September 27, 1805, Kroppenstaedt, Prussia
d. March 10, 1898, Bristol, England

George Müller

7 he son of a tax collector, George did not become a Christian until he was twenty years old. He was a habitual thief and accomplished liar, and said himself that there was almost no sin into which he hadn't fallen.

While attending Halle University, George was invited by his friend Beta to a prayer meeting. For the first time, George saw someone kneeling to pray. The singing, prayers, Bible study, and reading of a printed message reached his sinful heart. He wrote of that night, "On that evening, He began a work of grace in me, though I obtained joy without any deep sorrow of heart, and with scarcely any knowledge. That evening was the turning point in my life." The changes in himself that George had tried unsuccessfully to make through his own resolve were accomplished by his newfound love of Jesus.

George's practice of depending on God to meet his needs began in earnest when, as a newlywed, he took his first pastorate. Rejecting the practice of renting pews and accepting a fixed salary, George asked that a box be placed at the back of the church. Anyone who felt led to contribute to his support could do so. God not only provided for the Müller's needs, but also blessed them to be able to give to others. George's radical obedience and trust in God allowed him to be used in astonishing ways.

God used George to build five large orphanages that housed over two thousand orphans, plus a staff of two hundred. All the money and workers needed came as a direct result of prayer. No debts were ever incurred, and no appeals or requests for money were made. George received Ł1,500,000 in answer to his faith-filled prayers.

His personal income averaged around $12,000 a year. He kept about $1,800 to support his family and gave the rest away. George read the Bible through over two hundred times and reported some fifty thousand specific answers to prayer in his lifetime.

His life would have been remarkable enough in his care of over ten thousand orphans, but God chose to use George Müller to touch his world with the Gospel. In 1834, George founded the Scriptural Knowledge Institution, which was instrumental in supporting 163 missionaries and sending almost three hundred thousand Bibles around the world. He also started day schools for adults and children that educated over one hundred twenty-one thousand students, many of whom came to know the Lord.

At the age of seventy, George began his own missionary tours. In the next seventeen years, he traveled over two hundred thousand miles, went to forty-two different countries, and preached to over 3 million people.

Perhaps the greatest testimony to the power of God to accomplish great things through ordinary people is witnessed by the ongoing work of the George Müller Foundation. By continuing to care for the physical and spiritual needs of children, providing housing and a peaceful environment for many elderly, supporting missionaries and those involved in Christian education, and providing Christian literature throughout the world, the Foundation operates in accordance with the Christian principle affirmed by George Müller that "the provision comes by prayer and faith without anyone being asked, whereby it might be seen that God is faithful still and hears prayer still."[*]

---

[*] For further reading about George Müller, see *Release the Power of Prayer* (2000), published by Whitaker House.

Seven

Pardon for an Unrepentant People

M oses sent twelve spies to Canaan to bring back a report of the land. When they returned, ten said that, though the land was good, Israel would surely be defeated by the inhabitants. Although Joshua and Caleb argued that Israel certainly could drive out their enemies, the people moaned, complained, and rebelled, even seeking to stone Joshua and Caleb and return with new leaders to Egypt. The anger of the Lord was kindled against them and threatened to bring judgment. (See Numbers 13–14.)

Faithfully, once more Moses interceded:

> *I pray, let the power of the Lord be great, just as Thou hast declared, "The LORD is slow to anger and abundant in lovingkindness, forgiving iniquity and transgression; but He will by no means clear the guilty, visiting the iniquity of the fathers on the children to the third and the fourth generations."*
>
> (Num. 14:17–18)

Just as Abraham had prayed centuries before, Moses focused upon two things: the integrity of the Lord and His great mercy. When the Scripture says that God will *"by no means clear the guilty"* (v. 18), it speaks of those who sin but do not repent. Yet, even in such a circumstance, the Lord is able to be entreated.

Remember, the Israelites had rebelled; they were not even aware that their sin had placed them at the threshold of God's wrath. On one side, the Lord looked at a nation of unrepentant, sinful people, and on the other side, He saw one man, Moses, praying. Even though the prophet acknowledged that the Lord would not *"clear the guilty,"* Moses still prayed that God would forgive Israel:

> *Pardon, I pray, the iniquity of this people according to the greatness of Thy lovingkindness, just as Thou also hast forgiven this people, from Egypt even until now.*
>
> (Num. 14:19)

Note with awe the Lord's response to Moses' mercy prayer. He said, *"I have pardoned them according to your word"* (v. 20). Incredible!

Three million Israelites had not repented, nor rent their hearts, nor confessed their sins to God or one another. Not one of them who had sinned possessed a broken, contrite spirit. Yet the Lord said, *"I have pardoned them."* This response is utterly amazing to me. The Lord granted Israel forgiveness *"according to* [Moses'] *word."* Staggering!

One man with favor from God brought mercy upon 3 million people who had not repented.

Then, in case we might think this is some kind of easy grace, the Lord reaffirmed His purpose for all nations, beginning with Israel. He said, *"But indeed, as I live, all the earth will be filled with the glory of the LORD"* (v. 21).

The integrity of the Lord is nonnegotiable. He said, in effect, "Though I forgive, I am not going to change My plans. The world will be filled with My glory."

When we ask God for mercy, we are not asking Him to compromise His intentions or His standards. We are asking only that He forgive the sins of people, showing His mercy until He can fulfill His purpose. In truth, we are in complete agreement with His righteous judgments. We earnestly want His glory to overshadow North, South, and Central America; to roll through Europe, Africa, and Asia; to revive Israel and touch the Middle East, Australia, and the rest of the world. We shout a resounding "Yes!" to the purpose of God. "Fill our land with Your glory, Lord!"

But we also pray, "Until Your purposes are perfected, reveal Your mercy. Forgive, O Lord, the sins of Your people."

Do you need a vision of God's ultimate destiny for your nation? The voice of the Lord has promised, *"As I live, all the earth will be filled with [My] glory"* (Num. 14:21). Your nation, being part of the earth, is included in God's heart. He will hear our prayers for mercy as we reach, with Him, toward His ultimate goal.

Do you doubt this? The mercy prayer worked for Moses. God brought the first of His nations, Israel, from Egypt to Canaan, and He did so through the prayers and leadership of one man.

You say, "But that was Moses. I am a nobody." Jesus said, *"He who is least in the kingdom of heaven is greater than* [John the Baptist]" (Matt. 11:11). How can that be? We have the power of Christ's blood covenant to aid our quest for mercy!

Yes, God indeed used Moses to bring an imperfect people from promise to fulfillment. Whether we are praying for our nations, our cities, our churches, or our families, wherever we serve as leaders of people, the Lord will pardon them *"according to your word"* (Num. 14:20).

An Intercessor Is Committed

> *Then Moses returned to the LORD, and said, "Alas, this people has committed a great sin, and they have made a god of gold for themselves. But now, if Thou wilt, forgive their sin—and if not, please blot me out from Thy book which Thou hast written!"*
>
> (Exod. 32:31–32)

An intercessor gives up all personal advantage for the sake of those for whom he prays. Moses knew he had favor with God. Yet he presented himself as a remarkable portrait of one irreversibly committed to Israel's transformation. He said, *"If Thou wilt, forgive their sin—and if not, please blot me out from Thy book."*

Moses said, in effect, that he was not serving for individual gain or glory. This servant of the Lord could not be separated, blessed, honored, or pleased apart from the fulfillment of God's promise to Israel. If God would not forgive them, He could not have Moses either. Israel and Moses had become a package deal.

Have you struggled with situations in your personal life in which you cannot seem to break through? Perhaps you are spending too much time on *your* needs and not enough time praying for others. Make a prayer list of people with desperate needs, and as you intercede for them, see if the Holy Spirit doesn't break through for you, too. Remember the story of Job? When he prayed for his friends, God healed him. *Intercession not only transforms the world, but also transforms us.*

WHO IS STANDING IN THE GAP?

Moses accomplished what the Lord gave him to do. Through him, God brought the Israelites from Egypt to the Promised Land. The book of Psalms records the tremendous role Moses played in this epic event:

> *They made a calf in Horeb, and worshiped a molten image. Thus they exchanged their glory for the image of an ox that eats grass. They forgot God their Savior, who had done great things in Egypt, wonders in the land of Ham, and awesome things by the Red Sea. Therefore He said that He would destroy them, had not Moses His chosen one stood in*

*the breach before Him, to turn away His
wrath from destroying them.* (Ps. 106:19–23)

One man changed the mind of God.

But something else happened on that journey
that was not good for Moses. Let me set the scene.
Israel was thirsty. This time, instead of asking Moses
to strike the rock to bring water, the Lord told Moses
to speak to it. Angered at the people for their sin,
Moses struck the rock instead. This disobedient action disqualified Moses from entering the Promised
Land. (See Numbers 20:7–12.)

I have often pondered this situation. Moses went
so far, yet he could not go with Israel into Canaan.
Why? Then it occurred to me: it is possible Moses
couldn't enter the Promised Land because there was
no one praying for him in the hour of his sin.

Everyone needs someone who will pray for him.
You need to pray for your pastor, and pray for those
who intercede for others. Everyone has at least one
place in his heart that is not yet transformed, an
area that needs the intercession of Christ through a
friend on his behalf. Even Moses, intercessor for
millions, needed someone to pray and stand in the
breach of obedience for him.

*Lord Jesus, I am awed at Your willingness to
show mercy. You actually changed Your mind
about judgment on sinners because of one man,
Moses. Lord, in my world and times, let me be
that one who so delights You, who is so intimate
with You, that my prayer for mercy outweighs
Your judgment to destroy the disobedient. May*

the favor You have given to me be multiplied to those who yet do not know You, and may it spread until all the earth is filled with Your glory!

The Power of One Christlike Life...

John Bunyan
b. November 1628, Elstow, England
d. August 1688, London, England

John Bunyan

A tinker who sold and mended pots and pans was remarkably used by God to write books that would lead others to the Mender of broken hearts. After narrowly escaping from a near drowning and miraculously being saved from death when another soldier asked to take his guard duty, John Bunyan realized that God was preserving him from judgment and granting him mercy. He tried to clean up his own life, but miserably failed in his pursuit of a man-made piety. In despair, he decided that if he was going to be damned anyway, he might as well be "damned for many sins as for few."

He was rescued from this dangerous course when a woman, noted for bad character herself, accused him of being "the ungodliest fellow that ever she heard in all her life." Once again, he set out to mend his ways, and he changed so drastically that he began to think that "no man in England could please God better" than he. Outwardly changed, he was plagued by troublesome doubts.

Overhearing three Christian women talking about regeneration, Bunyan was drawn to their message. They directed him to speak with John Gifford, pastor of their small Baptist congregation. After conversations with the pastor and diligent study of the Scriptures, Bunyan found an assurance of his salvation.

A short while later, the pastor died, and the congregation asked Bunyan to assist with the preaching responsibilities at the church. Although the thought of preaching at first "dash[ed] and abash[ed]" his spirit, he agreed to their request. People came from all over the countryside to hear him preach Christ, "the sinner's friend, while sin's eternal foe."

In 1660, Bunyan was brought before a local magistrate and accused of holding services not in conformity with the Church of England. Although he had four young children by Margaret, his first wife, who had died, and Elizabeth, his second wife, was pregnant, he refused to give any assurance that he would stop preaching; consequently, he was put in jail. Elizabeth fought courageously for his release. After losing the baby from the strain of Bunyan's imprisonment, she traveled to London to petition the House of Lords for her husband's release. She was told to return to her county and present her request to the local magistrates. When asked by one of the judges if her husband would quit preaching, she answered, "My lord, he dares not leave preaching as long as he can speak."

Bunyan was to spend the next twelve years in prison, but he supported his family by making and selling shoelaces and by writing tracts and books. The words of those who tried to silence him are no longer remembered, but God used a willing servant to write classic books, such as *The Pilgrim's Progress, The Holy War,* and *The Life and Death of Master Badman,* that continue to encourage Christians on their spiritual journeys and point them in the direction of their heavenly home.[*]

---

[*] For further reading of John Bunyan's work, see *Visions of Heaven and Hell* (1998) and *Journey to Hell* (1999), both published by Whitaker House.

Eight

God Talking to God

We have been studying the influence that one mercy-motivated intercessor can have on the heart of God. We looked at Abraham and then expanded our study to Moses. We saw, with amazement, how the Lord heard and responded with redemption to the prayer for mercy. One person, Moses, stood between divine judgment and Israel's sin, and one person's intercession was enough to bring Israel from its confusion as a nation of oppressed, rebellious slaves toward the standard of spiritual attainment portrayed in the Old Testament. Let us revel in the power of prayer and the approachable heart of God.

Yet, even as we are awed by the power and mercy released through prayer, some of us, in the subconscious realms of our souls, find another thought forming. At first, it appears as a question. However, because it is often left unattended, for many it turns into a doubt. The problem is this: as we watch the cycle repeat itself again and again—of Israel's sin, of God's threatened wrath, and of Moses' plea for mercy—we are troubled. Is Moses, a mere man, more merciful than God?

The very idea seems blasphemous; we are instantly ashamed that we thought it, so we bury it. Yet, the fact is, for many, the doubt was buried alive and remains alive. For it is true that, had not Moses interceded, the Lord would have destroyed men, women, and children for one short period of sin. Moses does seem to be more merciful than God.

Of course, as good Christians, we dare not voice this doubt; we do not even whisper it to our most trusted friends. As a result, what ought to be a pure and wonderful example of the value and power of prayer, instead, on a more subconscious level, tempts us to mistrust God's goodness, using our doubts to excuse ourselves whenever our goodness fails.

Even if you are not personally struggling with this battle, someone you love probably is or will be. When people fall away from God, often it is because they have sinned and now doubt the Lord's goodness to forgive them.

Thus, we need to clear up this mystery concerning God's wrath. Why isn't God automatically merciful? Why does He warn of judgment, yet reveal Himself in mercy and restraint when even one intercessor pleads on behalf of others?

THE PURPOSE OF GOD

To answer these questions we must return to the first statements the Almighty made in Genesis concerning mankind; we must understand the reason for our existence. Let's read what God Himself declared in the sacred Scriptures as His purpose for mankind. The Lord said,

"Let Us make man in Our image, according to Our likeness."...And God created man in His own image, in the image of God He created him; male and female He created them.
                                    (Gen. 1:26–27)

The living God has encoded into humanity a grand and irreversible purpose: *man has been created to reveal the nature of God.* This has been the Lord's purpose from the beginning, and, though the world has continually changed, the Almighty has never deviated from this plan.

We should not assume that the creation of Adam and Eve, however, completed this purpose. Genesis marks a beginning, not a fulfillment. Although Adam and Eve possessed intelligence and freedom of will above that of the animals, God's plan was only initiated in Eden; they were still far from being in the image and likeness of God. Indeed, shortly after they were created, they fell into sin. If they were created in the likeness of God in their essence, how is it that they sinned? Sin is the one thing God cannot do.

Let's think of mankind as a singular person in search of his identity and destiny. For man, Eden is the commencement to a journey that can end only when man attains the image and likeness of God. Man discovers sin, but fulfillment is not there; he receives moral law and tries to obey it, but again, satisfaction eludes him. Having been born in paradise with God, man carries in his primordial soul the memory of paradise lost.

The introduction of Christ into the consciousness of mankind marks the beginning, in divine earnest, of

God's action to accomplish His original purpose with man. Christ not only provides payment for man's sins, but also sets the pattern for man's life.

As Christians we heartily agree with the payment of Christ. However, we only remotely accept the pattern He provides. We think the first aspect of our relationship with Christ, our forgiveness, was the goal. It is not. The first purpose is servant to the second. Christ forgives us so that He can transform us.

Man transformed into the image of Christ is the pinnacle truth, the supreme revelation, of God's will for humanity. No truth is more poignantly chronicled by Jesus and the New Testament writers. Every instruction of righteousness points us to the standard of Christ; every apostolic teaching prods us to fulfill Genesis 1:26–27 through the manifestation of Christ within us.

Paul wrote in Romans 8:29 that Christ is the Firstborn of many predestined brethren. Galatians 2:20 and 2 Corinthians 13:3 explain that Christ is living in us now, while 2 Corinthians 3:18 assures us that, from the moment Christ entered our spirits, as we behold Him, we each *are being transformed into the same image from glory to glory, just as from the Lord, the Spirit.*

We are born again, not just to go to heaven, but to become like Christ. We unite with other Christians, not only for administrative expediency, but also because Christ manifests Himself most perfectly through a many-membered body. We are part of a second Genesis whose goal is to fulfill the first Genesis: man in the image of God.

In scores of Scriptures, some so wonderful their truths will never be fully apprehended on earth, the Holy Spirit repeatedly proclaims the magnificent purposes of God in man. There will be a last trumpet when, with the pains of labor, our mortality will put on immortality (1 Cor. 15:51–53), and, beloved, we will be like Him (1 John 3:2)! At that moment, all heaven will celebrate in awe and praise, for *"the mystery of God is finished"* (Rev. 10:7). Man, in perfect submission to God, will bear His glory and power.

Adam never was the prototype. From eternity God's purpose was that man would be conformed to Jesus Christ, not Adam. God chose us in Christ prior to Adam's fall. Indeed, He chose us *"before the foundation of the world"* (Eph. 1:4).

God's purpose from the beginning was to make man in Christ's likeness. When we seek to know God's will, let us seek first to satisfy the call to Christlikeness. Yes, the maturation of this dimension of our lives abides in ascendant purity, far above every other aspect of our existence. Whom we will marry, where we will work, or what church we will attend are important decisions, but they are incomparable to what we become in the attainment of Christlikeness. The reason God created man is so that he would become like Jesus; it is the reason He created you.

LET US MAKE MAN

Yet we haven't fully addressed the relationship among God, man, and the power and purpose of prayer. All we have done is establish that God's goal in creating man was to reveal through him the nature of Christ. Let us, therefore, return to Genesis.

When speaking of the nature of God, the Scriptures proclaim the singularity of the Godhead: *"The LORD...our God, the LORD is one!"* (Deut. 6:4). The Scriptures nearly always refer to God in singular terms. From the beginning, we read that God (singular) created the physical world. But then, when we study His creation of man, we see that the Almighty speaks of Himself in plural terms, saying, *"Let Us make man in Our image"* (Gen. 1:26).

We define the Lord's ability to remain one in nature yet separate in manifestation as the Trinity. One clear example of this paradox is seen in the relationship between Jesus and His Father. Each time Christ prayed to the Father, it was, in truth, God on earth talking with God in heaven. Figuratively, we could say that God separated Himself, became God in two "places," yet remained one with Himself in nature.

Though Jesus Christ bears the likeness of man and represents mankind through the human side of His nature, spiritually He is of the same substance as God. Paul wrote that *"although* [Christ] *existed in the form of God,* [He] *did not regard equality with God a thing to be grasped, but emptied Himself"* (Phil. 2:6–7). He was *"begotten"* (Ps. 2:7) of the Father as He entered the realm of time, remaining one with the Father, yet separated organically from the Godhead by human flesh and subjective human experience. As Christians, we accept the mystery of the Trinity even if we cannot fully understand it.

However, this discovery of God's "separated oneness" leads us back to our original question concerning intercessory prayer and why it is able to restrain God's judgments or even cancel them completely. Specifically, what was it about Moses' prayer, the prayer of a solitary individual, that could obtain forgiveness for 3 million people who had not repented of their sins?

On the surface, Moses seems more merciful than God. But Moses is God's workmanship. Let's look at what God worked into His servant. We can imagine that the highly cultured Egyptians were shocked that Moses, now a mature and popular prince in Egypt, had become increasingly more concerned for the Hebrew slaves. After all, Moses was enjoying the finest conditions that civilization and position in life provided. He had nothing personal to gain, no advantage to be found by identifying himself with Egypt's slaves. Indeed, the Egyptians deemed the Israelites hardly more valuable than cattle. The idea of somehow helping the Hebrews was preposterous. Help them? As a prince in Egypt, Moses *owned* them!

Yet Moses could not defend himself against the deepening burdens of his own heart. Even against his will, empathy toward the Hebrews was growing within him. From the moment he began to identify with the weaknesses, injustices, and sufferings of his oppressed brothers, the Spirit of Christ set about to awaken him to his destiny. As I said earlier, this act of compassionate identification with those who are scorned, disgraced, or discredited is called the *"reproach of Christ,"* which Moses considered to be *"greater riches than the treasures of Egypt"* (Heb. 11:26).

The process of training, breaking, and reshaping continued in Moses for forty years. Until Christ began His work in him, Moses had been aloof and apathetic toward Israel's need, but with the advancement of Christ into his life, he became God's vehicle to bring and extend mercy to Israel.

Whenever we read of intercessory prayer or redemptive action on the part of one for the needs of many, whether in the Old or New Testament, it is actually Christ manifesting, inspiring, and empowering that individual. Moses bore Christ's reproach and was himself the expression of God's mercy toward Israel.

Therefore, the question of whether Moses was more merciful than God proves to be superfluous. For the spirit of intercession that emerged through Moses was not really Moses' spirit, but Christ's Spirit praying through him on man's behalf. This is significant: man, inspired by Christ, is the primary means through which God brings forth mercy to other men. What we are actually seeing operate through human instrumentality is God in His mercy interceding before God in His justice. At the highest level, intercessory prayer is God talking to God through man.

Remember my earlier statement that God separates Himself from Himself, yet never loses His essential oneness with Himself in the Godhead. When the Lord appears ready to reveal His wrath, He will always, simultaneously, be searching for an individual through whom Christ can emerge in the mercy prayer. The Almighty's primary goal is not to destroy wickedness but to use wickedness in the process of transforming man into the Redeemer's image. If threatening justifiable wrath awakens even one to manifest the mercy of Christ, that one transformed life is more valuable to the Almighty than His need to destroy wickedness.

Without doubt, God must reveal His righteous judgment concerning sin; otherwise, mercy has no meaning or value. God is revealed in the Godhead as Father, Son, and Holy Spirit. The Father is God manifesting Himself in authority and justice; Christ is God revealed in redemptive mercy; the Holy Spirit is God in manifest power, bringing forth in creative or destructive power the expressed will of the Godhead. The ultimate revelation of God is seen in the unveiling of perfect love; God's wrath is the backdrop. The display of this redemptive love in man is the purpose of man's existence.

Thus, as Christians, our call is to manifest the voice and mercy of Christ to God. In intercessory prayer and mercy-motivated action, we identify with those exiled from heaven because of sin; we unite with those who feel separated from God because of physical suffering, heartache, or persecution. In manifesting the redemptive mercy of God, we embrace the very reason for our existence: to be transformed into Christ's image.

MORE PERFECT THAN PARADISE

God is so committed to man's transformation that He limits much of the administration of mercy so that it can come only through human agencies. Yes, He provides a wonderful variety of life's gifts to all men, and He *"sends rain on the righteous and the unrighteous"* (Matt. 5:45). However, it is human beings who must feed the hungry and clothe the naked; the oppressed will likely remain so until a caring man or woman brings deliverance. The suffering in the world around us compels us either toward hardness of heart or compassion. This is the very nature of life itself: God's mercy enters this world through the narrow channel of the human will.

Thus, the Lord told Moses,

> *Behold, the cry of the sons of Israel has come to Me; furthermore, I have seen the oppression with which the Egyptians are oppressing them. Therefore, come now, and I will send you to Pharaoh.* (Exod. 3:9–10)

The Lord says, *"I have seen the oppression....I will send you."* God sees the need, but He reveals His mercy through His servant. So also with us. God sees the oppression and hears the cries of people, but His plan of mercy is to inspire us with Christ, who reaches through us to others. Whether we are speaking of Moses' intercession or the temple offerings of the Jewish priests or the most perfect act of intercession—Christ's incarnation and death—God's mercy finds its greatest manifestation through human instrumentality.

When we hear that the Spirit of God is threatening judgment, the very fact that He warns us gives us the opportunity, even with fear and trembling, to embrace the role of Christ-inspired intercession. God actually desires that we touch His heart with mercy, thus averting wrath. In truth, the primary reason God warns is not so that we can run and hide, but so that we can stand and pray. He seeks to inspire mercy in His people; otherwise, why would He create a world where He allows Himself to be entreated by prayer? Even when the Almighty shows Himself angered, grieved, or poised for judgment, He tells us that He is still seeking a means of mercy. He says, *"I* [am searching] *for a man among them who* [will]...*stand in the gap before Me for the land, that I should not destroy it"* (Ezek. 22:30).

We can expect that the Lord will thrust us into times of desperation in which genuine calamities or fearful situations loom ahead of us. He warns us so that we can be active participants with Him in the redemptive purpose. And it is in such cases, whether our cry is for our children or church, our city or country, that we are compelled toward God for mercy. For it is often in pure desperation that we grasp and attain the nature of Christ.

To turn and actually call for or demand divine judgment against people is to position ourselves in an attitude that is exactly opposite the heart God desires to reveal in us. Indeed, whenever we judge according to the flesh, there is only one thing we can be guaranteed, according to Jesus. He says, *"In the way you judge, you will be judged; and by your standard of measure, it will be measured to you"* (Matt. 7:2). In fact, God will often stop dealing with the one we are judging and start dealing with us if our attitude is anything but redemptive.

Now, let me state that there will be times when we are called to bring forth God's judgment, but there is a prerequisite. John wrote,

And we have come to know and have believed the love which God has for us. God is love, and the one who abides in love abides in God, and God abides in him. By this, love is perfected with us, that we may have confidence in the day of judgment; because as He is, so also are we in this world.

(1 John 4:16–17)

There are times when God brings forth judgment, not in the final sense, but in the immediacy of our world. The word *confidence* in this context means "free speech." In other words, not until *"love is perfected with us"* will we be qualified to speak God's wrath. Possessing God's love precedes proclaiming God's judgments. From a heavenly perspective, we have no authority to judge sin if we are not first willing to die for it.

Adam's failure and subsequent expulsion from Eden seemed the worst of all possible events. Yet from the Almighty's perspective, there were lessons man needed to learn about mercy that could not be taught in Paradise. Indeed, what looks like an imperfect environment to us is actually the perfect place to create man in the likeness of God. Here, we have a realm suitable for producing tested virtue. In this fallen world, character can be proven genuine and worship made pure and truly precious. Yes, it is here where we truly discover the depths of God's love in sending Christ to die for our sins. And here, in the fire of life-and-death realities, is where we become like Him.

Lord Jesus, Your love, Your sacrifice, is the pattern for my life. How I desire to be like You. I want more than anything to reveal Your mercy, both to the world and to the Father. I surrender all my other rights and privileges so that I may possess this glorious gift of conformity to You. I love You, Lord. Use me, pray through me, love through me, until, in all things, I reflect Your image and likeness.

The Power of One Christlike Life...

Saint Francis of Assisi
b. circa 1181, Assisi, Duchy of Spoleto
d. October 3, 1226, Assisi
canonized July 15, 1228

Saint Francis of Assisi

*B*aptized as Giovanni, Francesco di Pietro di Bernardone was renamed Francis by his father, who had been away in France buying cloth for the family business at the time of his son's birth. For the first twenty-five years of Francis's life, he lived exuberantly and was considered by his friends to be a master of revelry. Not until after being captured and imprisoned for nearly a year while fighting in Assisi's battle with the neighboring town of Perugia and then setting off again for battle in the papal army did Francis begin to turn to spiritual matters. On his way to war, Francis became sick and had to return home. During this time, he began to seek God's will for his life.

Stopping by a rundown chapel, Francis experienced a vision that would change the course of his life and the lives of countless others. He heard the voice of Jesus coming from the crucifix, saying, "Francis, go, repair my house, which, as you see, is falling completely to ruin."

Taking the message literally, Francis began to manually set about to repair that church as well as two others. Eventually, the full meaning of Christ's message impacted Francis's heart. Shedding the trappings of his material possessions, including the approval of his earthly father, Francis devoted himself to obeying the commands of his heavenly Father.

Denouncing wealth and embracing the cross and teachings of Christ, Francis preached a message that shocked some and drew others. Before long, two brothers began following Francis, and then their number increased to twelve. Francis sent the twelve out, two by two, and soon there were a thousand, and then five thousand. This was the humble beginning of the Franciscan Order. The simple but radical message of the Gospel was touching and changing lives. Francis's message was preached even to the animals, whom he called to join with man in the worship of their Creator.

Today there are more than one hundred thousand Franciscans in North America, and more than a million worldwide, dedicated to preaching, teaching, missionary work, and charitable outreaches. Certainly, the prayer of St. Francis was answered, "Lord, make me an instrument of your peace."

Nine

The Beloved

We have been talking about prayer, Christlikeness, and the future of our nations. I would like to continue that focus, but look at the manifestation of Christ on earth as it impacts the heart of God. There is something utterly pleasing to the Father when Christ is revealed. It actually goes far beyond not destroying the wicked; it fulfills the depths of His nature.

Thus, to satisfy God, we must perceive what the Son presents to the Father in terms of their relationship. Let us, therefore, consider first the weightiness of having Jesus Christ as our mediator with God.

Jesus says that the Father has loved Him from *"before the foundation of the world"* (John 17:24). The love that exists between the Father and the Son transcends the boundaries of time. Since before the ages began or the stars were young; before the earth, man, or angels were created, the Father and Son have known only love. Their union within the Trinity is so complete that, though they are two distinct persons, the Scripture can state with perfect fidelity, *"The LORD is our God, the LORD is one!"* (Deut. 6:4).

During His ministry, Jesus spoke frequently of this love between the Father and Himself. He said, *"The Father loves the Son, and has given all things into His hand"* (John 3:35). Again we read, *"For the Father loves the Son, and shows Him all things that He Himself is doing"* (John 5:20). And again, *"I love the Father, and as the Father gave Me commandment, even so I do"* (John 14:31).

We may read the Scriptures, but, without revelation, they seem two-dimensional. However, let us try to imagine what Jesus' baptism was really like. In His first public appearance, this love between Father and Son totally engulfed the scene at the river Jordan. While Jesus was still in the water,

> *heaven was opened, and the Holy Spirit descended upon Him in bodily form like a dove, and a voice came out of heaven, "Thou art My beloved Son, in Thee I am well-pleased."* (Luke 3:21–22)

Do not rush past this phrase: *"My beloved Son."* Jesus is not just "a son," or even "the Son"; He is the Father's *"beloved Son."* There is no one like Him. Here, in this incredible, inaugural moment, the Father Himself draws near. Almighty God moves from His throne in the highest heaven until His face is at the edge of our physical world. From eternity the Father speaks to His Son, *"In Thee I am well-pleased."*

Then, the Almighty turns and repeats nearly the same thought, only this time He is speaking to John the Baptist, the forerunner of Christ. The Father reveals, *"This is My beloved Son, in whom I am well-pleased"* (Matt. 3:17). Note that in both of the times He spoke, the Father could not help but express His love for Jesus. As was stated earlier, the Father is obsessed, literally consumed, with love for His Son.

We do not have a human reference to understand the energy, the passion, and the unrestrained oneness that exists between the Father and the Son. We can see faint reflections of it on earth; we watch in awe and learn of it. Within the love between the Father and Son is the essence of heaven; to taste it is to drink the nectar of eternal life.

"Beloved,...in Thee I am well-pleased" (Luke 3:22).

The deep, unfathomable perfection of God, the incomprehensible ethos of the divine nature, knows only pleasure in Jesus. The Almighty, who gives life to all, receives life from the Son. The Father gazes at His Son and harbors no slight shadow of regret, no lingering wish for someone or something better. In Christ, we behold God on earth satisfying God in heaven; we see perfect surrender in the embrace of perfect acceptance.

Their relationship is amazing. Add to it the fact that, prior to this encounter, Jesus had not accomplished any miracles; there were no signs or wonders, no vast multitudes. Outwardly, a carpenter named Jesus came to the Jordan, like everyone else, to be baptized. Until that moment, in the eyes of His contemporaries, Jesus' adult life was unremarkable. He was just another woodworker.

How was it that, even in the common tasks of an ordinary life, Jesus drew the praise of heaven? At the core of His being, He did only those things that pleased the Father. In everything, He stayed true, heartbeat to heartbeat, with the Father's desires. Jesus lived for God alone; God was enough for Him. Thus, even in its simplicity and moment-to-moment faithfulness, Christ's life was an unending fragrance, a perfect offering of incomparable love to God.

Privately, the unfolding stream of divine passion from the Father for Jesus never abated; the Jordan was but the first public exchange. We see other references as we proceed through the Scriptures. Look at Matthew's account in chapter 12. Christ's public ministry had begun. Notice how what was written from eternity past again describes their holy relationship. Many are following and He is healing them all, yet He bids the multitudes not to make Him known,

> *in order that what was spoken through Isaiah the prophet, might be fulfilled, saying, "BEHOLD, MY SERVANT WHOM I HAVE CHOSEN; MY BELOVED IN WHOM MY SOUL is WELL-PLEASED; I WILL PUT MY SPIRIT UPON HIM, AND HE SHALL PROCLAIM JUSTICE TO THE GENTILES."* (Matt. 12:17–18)

Carefully read the sacred text, the prophetic word chosen to describe the Father and His beloved. God cannot speak of Christ, or even inspire reference to Him, without calling Him *"MY BELOVED IN WHOM MY SOUL is WELL-PLEASED."*

One day, indeed, we will gaze upon the face of God's beloved and we will know that to see His face is the highest blessedness of heaven.

Again, look in Matthew 17. On the holy mountain Jesus was magnificently transfigured before three of His disciples. His face shone like the sun. His garments became white as light, flashing like lightning. Moses and Elijah appeared, talking with Christ. Into this splendor, Peter nervously postured an idea. While his words were still in his mouth, a radiant cloud formed and then overshadowed the disciples. Out from this living splendor, again, the voice of God was heard: *"This is My beloved Son, with whom I am well-pleased; listen to Him!"* (Matt. 17:5).

The all-knowing, all-wise God, the Creator of heaven and earth, in the only times He has ever spoken audibly to mankind, has said the same basic thing: *"This is My beloved Son."* In all the unlimited creativity of the mind of God, there is nothing more profound, no greater revelation, than to say, "Listen to Him!"

On each occasion that He speaks, the Father returns to glorifying His Beloved. We hear this information, we write it down, we think we grasp God's truth, but we do not. We underline, but we do not understand. Too quickly we seek to move to another insight, but the voice of God brings us back. In the Father's eyes, there is no other truth. We have not genuinely understood who Jesus is; otherwise, we would feel as the Father does.

THE FATHER'S LOVE IN US

This love within the Godhead is the symphony of the universe. It is what makes heaven heavenly.

Yet it is not enough that we should merely know of it. Even as we are awed by such all-consuming one-ness, Jesus asks that each of us, as His disciples, would be included in this holy hymn of heaven. He prays,

> *O righteous Father,....I have made Thy name*
> *known to them, and will make it known; that*
> *the love wherewith Thou didst love Me may*
> *be in them, and I in them.*   (John 17:25–26)

Jesus asks that the *"love wherewith Thou didst love Me may be in them."* He prays that the same love, the same overwhelming fulfillment that the Father has in His Son, may also be manifested in us. In other words, it is God's will that we become as to-tally consumed with Jesus as the Father is!

WHAT CHRIST PROVIDES

But this is a book about intercession. How, then, does the love between the Father and the Son add to our ability to intercede for those around us? What do we gain through the knowledge of their love?

To answer these questions, let me pose another question: what is it, uniquely, that the Father has found in the Son that so fulfills Him? I believe the Son's gift is this: Jesus presents to the Father the opportunity to satisfy His deepest passions and to reveal His highest glory, the nature of which is love.

We see this unveiled in Jesus' statement, *"For this reason the Father loves Me, because I lay down My life"* (John 10:17). The Son presents to the Father reconciliation between heaven and earth. He allows God to be revealed as He truly is—not as an unbending judge but as a loving Father.

Perhaps it is incomprehensible to us that God could suffer or feel pain, yet the Scriptures reveal that the Spirit of God relates in interactive union with this world. In His eternal nature, the Father sees man's end from the beginning. However, in His relationship with mankind's journey through time, the Scriptures are plain: the heart of God is open and vulnerable to the human condition.

We read that, in Noah's day, the Lord was *"grieved in His heart"* (Gen. 6:6). The Psalms reveal that Israel *"grieved Him in the desert"* (Ps. 78:40). The word *grieved* means "to worry, pain, or anger." What does heaven look like when the heart of God is grieved? We know that when a sinner repents, there is increased joy among angels (Luke 15:7, 10), but could it be that until sinners repent, there is actually grieving in heaven?

I pose this as a question, but it is not hard to see the answer. Consider that the book of Judges tells us of a time when the Lord *"could bear the misery of Israel no longer"* (Judg. 10:16). You see, there is much evidence to tell us that the living God participates vicariously in the suffering and heartaches of His people. He was never aloof from Israel's condition. Just as the Spirit hovered over the pre-Creation world, God brooded over Israel, being deeply involved until He was unable to *"bear the misery of Israel"* any longer and He delivered them.

Since mankind's fall, there has been a restless longing in the heart of God toward man. We perceive this longing behind the words in John's testimony, *"God so loved the world, that He gave His only begotten Son"* (John 3:16). Indeed, if we are unreconciled with someone we love, do we not also carry heartache until we are restored? By providing atonement for man's sins, Jesus heals the estrangement, the wound in the Father's heart, and then He extends that healing to man.

In his letter to the Colossians, Paul explained what Christ has done. He wrote,

> *And when you were dead in your transgressions and the uncircumcision of your flesh, He made you alive together with Him, having forgiven us all our transgressions, having canceled out the certificate of debt consisting of decrees against us and which was hostile to us; and He has taken it out of the way, having nailed it to the cross.*
>
> (Col. 2:13–14)

Mankind's unpayable debt is paid; God's incurable wound, healed. Not only do we have peace with God through the sacrifice of Christ, but also God has peace with us. Freed from the limitations of justice, now the Father can lavish His love without restraint upon His children.

Let us celebrate what Christ has done. The demands of divine wrath, which could not be settled by man, are fully settled by God Himself through Christ. Indeed, Jesus said, *"The kingdom of heaven may be compared to a certain king who wished to settle accounts"* (Matt. 18:23). This is God's heart, through Christ: He desires to settle accounts with mankind!

As long as we abide in mercy, the full panorama of divine mercy will remain open and fully active toward us and mankind's need in general. When we pray, "in Jesus' name," we are coming to the Father with the goal of mercy in mind. The announcement that we have come "in Jesus' name" signifies that we are representatives of Jesus' purpose, which is mercy and redemption, not judgment.

COME BOLDLY FOR MERCY!

The Father has never taken pleasure in the death of the wicked (Ezek. 33:11). The idea that He has enjoyed destroying sinners is a satanic slander that Christ came to dispel. His attitude toward mankind is exactly the opposite: His joy increases when sinners repent. Because Christ's sacrifice for sin has led hundreds of millions to repentance, Jesus has increased the Father's joy inestimably.

Because judgment is now atoned for in Christ, the Father has full freedom to consider every prayer for mercy. He no longer is constrained to decide between judgment and mercy: *"Mercy triumphs over judgment"* (James 2:13)!

The church can come boldly to the throne of God's grace and stand before the mercy seat in prayer for the world around us. This is what Jesus gives to the Father: perfect fulfillment of God's love, perfect fulfillment of His compassion, perfect unveiling of the highest glory of God.

In fact, the very inspiration to intercede is the result of Christ's working within us. As Christ is revealed through our intercession, wrath is delayed and divine mercy begins searching for the opportunity to triumph. When we pray, "God be merciful," we are not merely delaying His wrath; in truth, we are also delighting and fulfilling His heart for mercy!

Do you feel the Father's love for Jesus increasing in you? Christ brings heaven to earth and bids us to join Him in the redemptive purpose. To cover sin—not to condemn but rather to intercede—is to reveal the nature of Christ. Whenever Christ is revealed, mercy triumphs, and the Father is well-pleased.

Lord Jesus, I desire to join You in bringing pleasure to the Father. Forgive me for my shallowness and indifference. Help me to see in You the pattern of love that never ceases to bring pleasure to the Father. You are the fragrance that pleases God. Come forth in Your mercy, even through me, and make me a source of delight unto the Father. Thank You, Lord, for You are my beloved, too, and in You, I find the river of God's pleasure.

The Power of One Christlike Life...

Charles Grandison Finney
b. August 29, 1792, Warren, Connecticut, USA
d. August 16, 1875, Oberlin, Ohio, USA

Charles Grandison Finney

*W*hile studying law, Charles Finney frequently came across references to Scripture that were the basis of legal principles. His interest in law led him to buy a Bible, the first that he had ever owned. Not understanding all that he read, he would question the local Presbyterian minister, George W. Gale. For the next few years as Finney searched the Scriptures, he was confronted by his own sinfulness and lack of assurance regarding eternal life.

Pride kept him from directly seeking counsel from the local minister or elders. In the fall of 1821, he was stopped from going to the office when an inward voice confronted him with these questions: "What are you waiting for? Did you not promise to give your heart to God? Are you endeavoring to work out a righteousness of your own?"

Realizing his own inability to save himself, while seeing that salvation was to be found entirely in Jesus Christ, he purposed to accept Christ that day or, as he said in his autobiography, "die in the attempt."

Still struggling with pride, he headed toward the woods where he could pray unobserved. Rustling leaves and the fear of being seen distracted him from his purpose. Finally, in desperation, his pride was broken, and he heard God's voice speaking to him: *"Then shall ye call upon me, and ye shall go and pray unto me, and I will hearken unto you. And ye shall seek me, and find me, when ye shall search for me with all your heart"* (Jer. 29:12–13 KJV). Finney realized that his faith had been solely intellectual; at that moment, he placed his trust in God and took Him at His Word.

For the rest of the morning, the Lord opened His promises to Finney, and he "took hold of them and fastened upon them with the grasp of a drowning man." As he made his way back to the village, though, Finney was struck with the fear that he had grieved the Holy Spirit because he no longer felt conviction for his sins. Instead, he experienced an unspeakable peace of mind.

As he returned to work that day, he stayed in a spirit of tranquility. That evening as he went into the back office to pray, the room was lit by the glory of the Lord. Finney wept aloud and seemed to bathe the Lord's feet with his tears. Without any expectation, he received a "mighty baptism of the Holy Spirit" that came over him "in waves of liquid love." Literally bellowing, he cried out, "I will die if these waves continue to pass over me! Lord, I cannot bear any more!"

A choir member came by and found him weeping. Asking if Finney was in pain, Finney replied, "No, but so happy that I cannot live." A rather serious-minded elder who stopped by that evening was moved to joyful laughter as Finney told him what had happened that day; a young man, who had slipped into the room and was listening to Finney's account, fell on the floor in a great agony of conviction, saying, "Pray for me!" Throughout the rest of the night, Finney would fall asleep and then awaken with an overwhelming sense of God's love. His guilt over past sins was gone forever, and he experienced the reality of being justified by faith in Christ.

The next day when a man whose case was to be heard came to ask Finney if he was ready to represent him, Finney replied, "I have a retainer from the Lord Jesus Christ to plead His cause, and I cannot plead yours." From that time on, Finney was impressed with the urgency to preach the Gospel. Hundreds of thousands were converted as a result of his evangelistic campaigns.

Finney was not only a great revivalist but also a pastor, teacher of theology, and president of Oberlin College. His skill in arguing cases before juries now was employed in persuading men, women, boys, and girls to *"come to the knowledge of the truth"* (1 Tim. 2:4) of the life-changing Gospel.[*]

---

[*] For further reading on Finney's life, see *Holy Spirit Revivals* (1999), published by Whitaker House.

Ten

The Gift of Woundedness

The world and all it contains was created for one purpose: to showcase the grandeur of God's Son. In Jesus, the nature of God is magnificently and perfectly revealed; He is the *"expressed image"* of God (Heb. 1:3). Yet to gaze upon Christ is also to see God's pattern for man. As we seek to be like Him, we discover that our need was created for His sufficiency. We also see that, once the redemptive nature of Christ begins to triumph in our lives, mercy begins to triumph in the world around us.

How will we recognize revival when it comes? Behold, here is the awakening we seek: men and women, young and old, all conformed to Jesus. When will revival begin? It starts the moment we say "yes" to becoming like Him; it spreads to others as Christ is revealed through us.

Yet to embrace Christ's attitude toward mercy is but a first step in our spiritual growth. The process of being transformed calls us to deeper degrees of transformation. Indeed, just as Jesus learned obedience through the things that He suffered (Heb. 5:8), so also must we. And it is here, even while we stand in intercession or service to God, that He gives us the *gift* of woundedness.

"Gift?" you ask. Yes, to be wounded in the service of mercy and, instead of closing our hearts, allow woundedness to crown love, is to release God's power in redemption. The steadfast prayer of the wounded intercessor holds great sway upon the heart of God.

We cannot become Christlike without experiencing woundedness. You see, even after we come to Christ, we carry encoded within us preset limits concerning how far we will go for love, and how much we are willing to suffer for redemption. The wounding exposes those human boundaries and reveals what we lack of His nature.

The path narrows as we seek true transformation. Indeed, many Christians fall short of Christ's stature because they have been hurt and offended by people. They leave churches discouraged, vowing never again to serve or lead or contribute because, when they offered themselves, their gift was marred by unloving people. To be struck or rejected in the administration of mercy can become a great offense to us, especially as we are waiting for, and even expecting, a reward for our good efforts.

Yet wounding is inevitable if we are following Christ. Jesus was both *"marred"* (Isa. 52:14) and *"wounded"* (Zech. 13:6), and if we are sincere in our pursuit of His nature, we will suffer as well. How else will love be perfected?

Let us beware. We either become Christlike and forgive, or we enter a spiritual time warp where we abide continually in the memory of our wounding. Like a systemic disease, the hurtful memories destroy every aspect of our reality. In truth, apart from God, the wounding that life inflicts is incurable. God has decreed that only Christ in us can survive.

Intercessors live on the frontier of change. We are positioned to stand between the needs of man and the provision of God. Because we are the agents of redemption, Satan will always seek the means to offend, discourage, silence, or otherwise steal the strength of our prayers. The wounding we receive must be interpreted in light of God's promise to reverse the effects of evil and make them work for our good (Rom. 8:28). Since spiritual assaults are inevitable, we must discover how God uses our wounds as the means to greater power. This was exactly how Christ brought redemption to the world.

Jesus knew that maintaining love and forgiveness in the midst of suffering was the key that unlocked the power of redemption. Isaiah 53:11 tells us, *"By His knowledge the Righteous One, My Servant, will justify the many, as He will bear their iniquities."*

Jesus possessed "revelation knowledge" into the mystery of God. He knew that the secret to unleashing world-transforming power was found at the cross. The terrible offense of the cross became the place of redemption for the world. Yet, remember, Jesus calls us to a cross as well. (See Matthew 16:24.) Wounding is simply an altar upon which our sacrifice to God is prepared.

Listen again to Isaiah's prophetic description of Jesus' life. His words, at first, seem startling, but as we read, we discover a most profound truth concerning the power of woundedness. He wrote,

But the LORD was pleased to crush Him, putting Him to grief; if He would render

> *Himself as a guilt offering, He will see His*
> *offspring, He will prolong His days, and the*
> *good pleasure of the LORD will prosper in*
> *His hand.*   (Isa. 53:10)

How did Jesus obtain the power of God's pleasure and have it prosper in His hands? During His times of crushing, woundedness, and devastation, instead of retaliating, He rendered Himself *"as a guilt offering."*

The crushing is not a disaster; it is an opportunity. You see, our purposeful love may or may not touch the sinner's heart, but it always touches the heart of God. We are crushed by people, but we need to allow the crushing to ascend as an offering to God. The far greater benefit is the effect our mercy has on the Father. If we truly want to be instruments of God's good pleasure, then it is redemption, not wrath, that must prosper in our hands.

So, when Christ encounters conflict, even though He is the Lion of Judah, He comes as the Lamb of God. Even when He is outwardly stern, His loving heart is always mindful that He is the *"guilt offering."* Thus, Jesus not only asks the Father to forgive those who have wounded Him, but also numbers Himself with the transgressors and intercedes for them (Isa. 53:12). He does this because the Father takes *"no pleasure in the death of the wicked"* (Ezek. 33:11), and it is the pleasure of God that Jesus seeks.

Is this not the wonder and mystery, yes, and the power, of Christ's cross? In anguish and sorrow, wounded in heart and soul, still He offered Himself for His executioners' sins. Without visible evidence of success, deemed a sinner and a failure before man, He courageously held true to mercy. In the depth of terrible crushing, He let love attain its most glorious perfection. He uttered the immortal words, *"Father, forgive them; for they do not know what they are doing"* (Luke 23:34).

Christ could have escaped. He told Peter as the Romans came to arrest Him, *"Do you think that I cannot appeal to My Father, and He will at once put at My disposal more than twelve legions of angels?"* (Matt. 26:53). In less than a heartbeat, the skies would have been flooded with thousands of warring angels. Yes, Jesus could have escaped, but mankind would have perished. Christ chose to go to hell for us rather than return to heaven without us. Instead of condemning mankind, He rendered *"**Himself** as a guilt offering"* (Isa. 53:10, emphasis added). He prayed the mercy prayer, *"Father, forgive them"* (Luke 23:34).

Jesus said, *"He who believes in Me, the works that I do shall he do also"* (John 14:12). We assume He meant that we would work His miracles, but Jesus did not limit His definition of *"works"* to the miraculous. The works He did—the redemptive life, the mercy cry, the identification with sinners, rendering Himself a guilt offering—*all* the works He did, we will *"do also."*

Thus, because He lives within us, we see that Isaiah 53 does not apply exclusively to Jesus; it also becomes the blueprint for Christ in us. Indeed, was this not part of His reward, that He would see His offspring (Isa. 53:10)? Beloved, *we* are the progeny of Christ.

Read these words from Paul's heart:

Now I rejoice in my sufferings for your sake,
and in my flesh I do my share on behalf of
His body (which is the church) in filling up
that which is lacking in Christ's afflictions.
(Col. 1:24)

What did the apostle mean? Did not Christ fully pay mankind's debts once and for all? Did Paul imply that *we* now take *Jesus'* place? No, we will never take Jesus' place. It means that Jesus has come to take our place. The Son of God manifests all the aspects of His redemptive, sacrificial life through us. Indeed, *"as He is, so also are we in this world"* (1 John 4:17).

Paul not only identified with Christ in his personal salvation, but he was also consumed with Christ's purpose. He wrote, *"That I may know Him, and the power of His resurrection and the fellowship of His sufferings, being conformed to His death"* (Phil. 3:10).

What a wondrous reality is the *"fellowship of His sufferings."* Here, in choosing to yoke our existence with Christ's purpose, we find true friendship with Jesus. This is intimacy with Christ. The sufferings of Christ are not the sorrows typically endured by mankind; they are the afflictions of love. They bring us closer to Jesus. United with Him, we increase the pleasure of God.

Father, I see You have had no other purpose in
my life but to manifest through me the nature of

Your Son. I receive the gift of woundedness. In response, in surrender to Christ, I render myself an offering for those You've used to crush me. May the fragrance of my worship remind You of Jesus, and may You forgive, sprinkle, and cleanse the world around me.

The Power of One Christlike Life...

Dietrich Bonhoeffer
b. February 4, 1906, Breslau, Germany
d. April 6, 1945, Flossenbürg concentration camp, Germany

Dietrich Bonhoeffer

*D*ietrich Bonhoeffer spent his formative childhood years in the twilight of the golden age of Germany before World War I. He grew up in the secure atmosphere of a loving family who believed in education, independent thinking, and serving one's country.

His father and older brothers were interested in science and law, but Dietrich took after his mother with interests in literature and the arts. Seeking to make his mark in a field distinct from his father and brothers, he chose to become a theologian when he was only fourteen years old. Although he apparently had a genuine faith as a child, his ambition to make a name for himself pushed this to the background. Graduating with distinction with a doctorate in theology when he was only twenty-one, Dietrich was too young to become a university professor, so he traveled to the United States for a year of additional studies at Union Theological Seminary in New York City.

Dietrich was an extremely intelligent and friendly young man. He was a private person but made friends easily because of his abilities in sports and music, his interest in new people and experiences, and his sense of humor. At Union, Dietrich became friends with Frank Fisher, a black fellow student who was interning at the Abyssinian Baptist Church in Harlem. Through his friendship with Frank, Dietrich saw the effects of institutionalized racism and experienced firsthand the faith and strength of the black community.

Another friend at Union was Jean Lasserre, a French pastor. Because of the historical animosity between Germany and France, this friendship took a little time to develop, but it became a strong and important one. In Jean, Dietrich was introduced to someone who read the Bible and applied it to his everyday life. He was challenged by Jean's pacifist beliefs, based on the Sermon on the Mount.

The influence of these two friendships and Dietrich's own growing personal faith helped to set the course of his life. He returned to Germany just as Adolf Hitler was coming to power in the early 1930s. Somewhere during his year at Union or just afterward, "the theologian became a Christian," according to his biographer. The Bible and the importance of the church as the true body of Christ came alive to him. He carried his experiences with Frank and Jean back with him to Germany as he related the struggle of blacks in America to the plight of the Jews and the Christians who opposed Hitler, and as he pondered how best to resist Nazism through pacifist methods.

Dietrich and his entire family were opposed to Hitler from the start and began working to stop the spread of Nazism. Dietrich concentrated his efforts in trying to prevent Nazi ideology from taking over the minds and hearts of those in the German national church. When much of the established church in Germany embraced Hitler's policies, Dietrich was involved in the formation and spiritual leadership of what became known as the Confessing Church, helping to draft statements of faith and becoming one of the directors of the Church's seminaries, which were carried on even after they were declared illegal by the Gestapo.

Against the backdrop of the church struggle in Germany, Dietrich wrote two classic works of theology that reflected his growing understanding of his faith, *Life Together* and *The Cost of Discipleship.*

He also pastored churches in England and traveled to other countries to tell the church worldwide what was happening in Germany. Because of his activities, he was eventually barred from writing, speaking, and living in Berlin, and had to report to the Gestapo.

When, for a variety of reasons, the Confessing Church lost its influence against Nazism, Dietrich made an excruciatingly difficult decision to join the German resistance movement in its plot to forcibly remove or kill Hitler. Even though he still held pacifist convictions and believed any killing was sinful, he felt he would be guilty of worse sin if he did nothing directly to attempt to stop the slaughter of the Jews.

Through the influence of his brother-in-law, who was working in the resistance under cover of the Abwehr, the German military intelligence organization, Dietrich was brought into the Abwehr and worked as a double agent by serving as the resistance's liaison to the Allies. In addition, he was involved in smuggling Jews out of Germany. It was this activity that led to his arrest and imprisonment. Other family members were also arrested as the Nazi authorities tried to discover the extent of their activities.

Dietrich spent two years in prison, during which he prepared for his trial, continued to write (much of his correspondence was later published as the highly acclaimed *Letters and Papers from Prison*), and carried on resistance work through the help of family and friends. With the failure of the July 20, 1944, bomb plot against Hitler and the resulting investigation, Dietrich and his family were implicated as members of the resistance. Just weeks before the end of the war, an outraged Hitler ordered the deaths of Dietrich and other family members. Dietrich was hanged at the Flossenbürg concentration camp, and his death was mourned by friends and associates all over the world.

His brother and two brothers-in-law were also executed.

Dietrich Bonhoeffer was a rare combination of brilliant theologian and deeply devoted follower of Christ who always sought to put his faith into practical action. His writings had a significant influence on theology in the twentieth century, and there is great interest in his life and works today. His stand against Hitler and his deep commitment to Christ combine to create a striking legacy, showing how one person can affect the course of the church, the nations, and the world.

Eleven

He Will Sprinkle Many Nations

S landered and rejected by men, Jesus appeared to be a failure. Suffering unspeakable pain, He remained true to redemption. He prayed the mercy prayer, the veil in the temple was torn in two, and the debt mankind owed to God was paid in full as mercy triumphed over judgment.

Let us now consider the reach of God's grace. Christ not only secured the pleasure of God for us but also God's power, which is strong enough to cleanse and turn nations to God. Isaiah 53 is preceded by a grand announcement that heralds the effects of Christ's victory. It reads:

> *Behold, My servant will prosper, He will be high and lifted up, and greatly exalted. Just as many were astonished at you, My people, so His appearance was marred more than any man, and His form more than the sons of men. Thus He will sprinkle many nations, kings will shut their mouths on account of Him; for what had not been told them they will see, and what they had not heard they will understand.* (Isa. 52:13–15)

What does it mean that He will *"sprinkle many nations"*? Under the old covenant, priests would take the blood of a sacrificed animal and, with it, sprinkle the temple and its furnishings. By so doing, they cleansed and made holy what was otherwise common and unclean.

In the New Testament, every believer serves as a priest before the throne of God (Rev. 1:6). Our quest is not merely to cleanse the temple, but also to see this promise fulfilled: the Lamb will sprinkle many nations; kings will see and understand.

WOUNDED INTERCESSORS FOLLOW THE LAMB

Our call is to follow the Lamb through our personal woundedness into the triumph of love and redemption. In the area of woundedness, we do not ask for wrath, but for mercy. Whatever injustice is hurled against us—slander, unfaithfulness, desertion, rejection, racism, or abuse—we render ourselves to God as the guilt offering. The greater the pain in releasing and forgiving the sins against you, the purer your love becomes. Remember, the prayer of the wounded intercessor holds great sway upon God's heart.

What we become in our individual conformity to Christ may be, in its own way, even more important to God than the revival for which we are praying. Listen, my friends. Just as mankind will look upon Him whom they pierced, and Christ's wounds will be with Him forever (Zech. 12:10), so *our* wounds will be recognized for what they are: entry points through which Christ's *"eternal weight of glory"* (2 Cor. 4:17) flows through us.

In speaking both of the sprinkling of the nations and the manifestation of the Redeemer's life, Isaiah presented a question. He asked, *"Who has believed our message? And to whom has the arm of the LORD been revealed?"* (Isa. 53:1). I write as one who has believed the report. Christ is *"the Lamb...who takes away the sin of the world!"* (John 1:29). I am committed to seeing His blood sprinkle and cleanse many nations; I am willing to follow the Lamb wherever He goes.

LET MERCY TRIUMPH

The Scriptures tell us that love *"bears all things, believes all things, hopes all things, endures all things. Love never fails"* (1 Cor. 13:7–8). If you will, in truth, hope and believe all things, you will also be called to bear and endure all things. Yet our hope is that love never fails. Yes, when Christ is revealed through the church, the power of redemption will prevail for our land, and mercy will certainly triumph over judgment.

Lord Jesus, for You I live; to be like You, may I be willing to die. Let redemption exult through me! Let mercy triumph through me! Do not allow me to withdraw from the fire of conformity to You. Create me in Your holy image; let love prevail through me!

The Power of One Christlike Life...

Watchman Nee
b. November 4, 1903, Swatow, China
d. June 1, 1972, Shanghai, China

Watchman Nee

*N*ee Shu-Tsu, meaning "he who proclaims his ancestors' merits," was born in answer to his mother's prayers. After having delivered two girls, she was afraid that she would not produce a male heir, thus disgracing her family. She promised God that if she had a boy, she would dedicate him to His service. God answered her prayers, and as Shu-Tsu grew older and his abilities developed, his mother suggested a new name for him, To-Sheng, which means "the sound of a gong." His new name would remind him and others that he was to be a bell ringer, or Watchman, calling others to serve God.

In spite of his mother's guidance and his education in an Anglican school, Watchman said that he "never imagined for a moment that [he] would become a preacher." He regarded the profession "as trifling and base." It was his mother's humility, though, in asking for his forgiveness for punishing him for an act that he had not done that reached his heart.

That evening, April 29, 1920, he sat in his room, struggling with the decision to accept or reject Christ. On one hand, he saw the enormity of his own sins, but then he was impressed with Christ's ability to forgive them. As he thought of Christ on the cross, he saw His outstretched hands welcoming him, and he heard the Lord say, "I am waiting here to receive you." From that moment, he became concerned about leading other people to his Savior.

Watchman attended the Bible Institute in Shanghai run by Dora Yu, and at the suggestion of a missionary, he made a list of seventy friends whom he prayed for daily. Miss M. E. Barber, another missionary, taught him about the filling of the Holy Spirit. After he was willing to give up his relationship with Chang Pin-huei, who at the time was not a Christian, and pray with conviction the words of Psalm 73:25, *"Whom have I in heaven but Thee? And besides Thee, I desire nothing on earth,"* Watchman Nee was filled with the Holy Spirit. Not only did his ministry then begin to expand but also all but one of the seventy friends for whom he was praying came to accept the Lord as their Savior.

Blessed with a photographic memory, Watchman read everything he could about the Christian faith. As a result, he was influenced by such writers as Jessie Penn-Lewis, George Müller, F. B. Meyer, Andrew Murray, Madame Guyon, and the writings of many of the Plymouth Brethren. He also read and studied the lives of great Christians. Above all, he was a student of the Scriptures; consequently, he became a man of great spiritual stature.

While experiencing a serious bout with tuberculosis, from which he was not expected to recover, Watchman Nee worked zealously to compile the truths that God had taught him. Amazingly, he recovered and was able to finish a three-volume work entitled *The Spiritual Man.*

In 1927, he began meeting with a group of Christians in a home in Shanghai. This became the first church founded on Nee's principles of locality, unity, and lay leadership. He believed that each community should have one place of worship and that denominational divisions were not scriptural.

Watchman Nee was arrested on April 10, 1952, by the Communist government and imprisoned for his faith. He served twenty years at Shanghai First Municipal Prison. In spite of his imprisonment, his teachings and writings continue to have a profound effect on the spread of local churches in and outside of China. His voluminous writings remain a source of spiritual growth and insight for many believers.[*]

---

[*] For further reading from the writings of Watchman Nee, see *Secrets to Spiritual Power* (1998), published by Whitaker House.

Twelve

A World in Revival and Harvest

We all know what the world looks like today. Immorality is rampant; abortion, legal; violence, a way of life. Many of the nations we are praying for are considered by sociologists to be in a "post-Christian" era, but I like to consider them in a "pre-revival" condition. Picture your nation on fire for God and the impact it will have on civilization.

I do not mean a revival merely of emotional religion, but a deep revival, born of genuine Christlikeness in the church. Picture your country experiencing a Christ awakening, where a priesthood of mature believers joins the Lamb before the throne of God's grace; where the Lamb is presented as a sacrifice for sin; and where many nations, according to Scripture, are sprinkled and cleansed (Isa. 52:15).

Do not say that it cannot happen. Look at Argentina; consider regions of China and Africa. Imagine your country leading many nations in reconciliation and healing, holiness, and the fear of the Lord among the people. Think of the multitudes of non-Christian peoples you would reach with the love of Jesus. Envision a hundred thousand loving, praying missionaries, empowered by the Holy

Spirit, being sent from your land to heal and encourage surrounding nations on every level of society.

We can go the way of the judgmental and critical. We can listen to those without vision who, like Samson, seek to pull our lands down upon themselves and their enemies. Or we can become Christlike and see a worldwide harvest before Jesus comes.

Remember, God is not looking impatiently at His watch; He is listening to His heart. He takes no pleasure in the death of the wicked (Ezek. 33:11); He desires for all men to be saved (2 Pet. 3:9). He has made provision for all men at the cross (Col. 1:20). He has inspired revival before. He can do it again.

Do you remember the story of the demonized boy whose father pleaded with Jesus for help? Feeling defeated, the man approached Christ. He was almost hopeless, weary with fighting to keep the boy alive after repeated demonic attacks. The man asked Jesus, *"If You can do anything, take pity on us and help us!"* (Mark 9:22).

Our attitude is often like that of this man. Our shoulders are hunched from fasting, and we are wearied with the fight. We come to the Lord looking for pity instead of power; we're seeking comfort instead of conviction to take a stand for our land.

To ask for mere pity from a God who has given us *"everything pertaining to life and godliness"* (2 Pet. 1:3) is an insult. Jesus retorted, *"'If You can!' All things are possible to him who believes"* (Mark 9:23).

ALL THINGS ARE POSSIBLE!

Let Christ's words become our battle cry. *"With God,"* Jesus said, *"All things are possible"* (Matt.

19:26). Lay aside the weight of unbelief; there is a race to be run, and we can win it. Ask God for more love, for love *"believes all things, hopes all things, endures all things"* (1 Cor. 13:7).

We are in the season of the miraculous. Just a few years ago, who would have thought that the USSR would fall and millions would come to Christ in that nation? Who would have predicted that hundreds of millions would have come to Christ just in the last ten years?

As I said earlier, I serve the Lord in the United States. After listening to those who said this nation was doomed, who would have thought that we would see such major decreases in crime, divorce, abortion, and teen pregnancy? Today, there is a resurgence of moral values on college campuses around the United States. Did we expect this good news? Did we anticipate that a deep and wonderful revival would hit the sports world so that hundreds of Christian athletes would become role models for our youth or that whole teams would huddle together in public prayer after games?

Who saw ten years ago that the church in America would be uniting in prayer? Or that reconciliation between races and denominations would begin in earnest? Or that nearly a million and a half men would stand in repentance for America at our nation's capital? These things happening in my land are a mere sign of the good things to come. Greater things can happen in your country. It would be just like the Lord to take your nation and pour out His Spirit upon it!

Daniel said, *"The people who know their God will display strength and take action"* (Dan. 11:32).

He went on to say, *"Those who have insight will shine brightly like the brightness of the expanse of heaven, and those who lead the many to righteousness, like the stars forever and ever"* (Dan. 12:3). It is not a time for fear, but faith. We do not need to come as beggars to Christ for pity; He is extending to us His power through our prayers, as long as we don't give up.

No Time for Discouragement

Have you heard the story of the man who was driving home from work one day and stopped to watch a local Little League baseball game in a park near his home? He sat down behind the bench on the first baseline and asked one of the boys what the score was.

"We're behind fourteen to nothing," the little boy answered with a smile.

"Really?" he said. "I have to say you don't look very discouraged."

"Discouraged?" the boy asked with a puzzled look on his face. "Why should we be discouraged? We haven't been up to bat yet."

It is not time to be discouraged. I believe the Devil has run up the score, but really, we haven't been to bat yet. For much of the past thirty years, we have been playing a poor defense to the Devil's initiatives (some of us haven't even been playing, but sitting quietly on the bench). But, my friends, the Devil's turn is nearly over; the church is getting ready to step up to the batter's box.

I make no apologies for believing as I do. Even if your country briefly turns darker spiritually, I am

fully convinced that, if the church will reveal the nature of Christ, *"nations will come to your light, and
kings to the brightness of your rising"* (Isa. 60:3).
Yes, the church in the image of Christ can delay
God's wrath and release revival in your land.

> *Father, forgive me for my unbelief. Forgive me
> for thinking that my one life cannot touch and
> awaken pleasure in Your heart. Father, my pur-
> suit will forever be to see Christ glorified within
> me. Let the nations experience the power of Your
> love for Jesus. Let Your church embrace the
> power of a Christlike life.*

The Power of One Christlike Life...

John Wesley
b. June 17, 1703, Epworth, Lincolnshire, England
d. March 2, 1791, London, England

John Wesley

*D*ramatically rescued at age six from the burning rectory of his father's Anglican parish, John Wesley had the hand of God upon him from his earliest years. While attending Oxford University, John took over the leadership of a group of men, which included George Whitefield, who met for prayer, Bible study, and daily communion. Because of their zealous compassion for the poor, they engaged in many charitable activities. This group came to be called "the Holy Club," or "Methodists," because of their methodical approach to holy living.

In 1725, John and his brother Charles sailed to the colony of Georgia in North America to serve as spiritual leaders for the colonists and to evangelize the American Indians. While traveling there, a storm arose on the sea, and John was deeply impressed by the peace and calmness of some Moravian missionaries. After less than satisfactory results among the Indians, the brothers returned to England. On his voyage home, John wrote, "I went to America to convert the Indians, but oh, who shall convert me?"

When he returned to England, John continued to preach, but the results were discouraging. Peter Bohler, a Moravian friend, invited John to a meeting on Aldersgate Street. John went unwillingly, but it was at that service that John's heart was "strangely warmed," and he felt assurance of his salvation. He began to preach with a new zeal. Whitefield invited him to come to Bristol to preach in the open air. Although prior to that time, he "thought the saving of souls almost a sin if it had not been done in a church," he was convinced by the marvelous results. That was the beginning of the Methodist Revival, which impacted not only Great Britain but other nations as well.

Known for his generosity, Wesley lived simply and gave away all he could to help the poor. Always concerned with social issues, he published grammars and dictionaries, pioneered educational reform, wrote and distributed tracts, founded orphanages and lending libraries, and established a dispensary at a foundry. He wrote a practical book on basic medicine, advocated changes in the law, denounced slavery and abuses within the church, and sought for improvements in prisons.

He even acknowledged the right for women to proclaim the Gospel, which was an unthinkable position in the Anglican Church. He wrote to Mary Bosanquet, one of the first Methodist women preachers, saying, "I think the strength of the cause rests...on your having an extraordinary call." He realized that what was occurring in the formation of Methodism was an "extraordinary dispensation" of God's activity; therefore, he was not surprised when he saw God moving in new and dramatic ways.

John Wesley was an expert organizer. He gathered converts into societies that met weekly for fellowship and spiritual accountability. Still an ordained priest in the Church of England, John encouraged the societies to maintain their allegiance to the Anglican Church. The "enthusiasm" of these Christians was not highly regarded in the established church, and as a result, the Methodist church was formed out of necessity rather than intention.

John traveled constantly, often as much as 8,000 miles a year on horseback. He seldom preached less

THE Power OF ONE CHRIST-LIKE LIFE

Francis Frangipane

Whitaker House

Unless otherwise noted, Scripture quotations are taken from the
New American Standard Bible (NAS), © 1960, 1962, 1968, 1971,
1973, 1975, 1977 by The Lockman Foundation. Used by
permission. Scripture quotations marked (KJV) are taken from the
King James Version of the Bible. Scripture quotations marked
(NKJV) are taken from the *New King James Version*, © 1979,
1980, 1982 by Thomas Nelson, Inc. Used by permission.
All rights reserved.

THE POWER OF ONE CHRISTLIKE LIFE

Francis Frangipane
In Christ's Image Training
125 Robins Square Ct.
Robins, IA 52328–9650
www.inchristsimage.org
Resources: 877.363.6889

ISBN-13: 978-0-88368-628-7
ISBN-10: 0-88368-628-7
Printed in the United States of America
© 1999, 2000 by Francis Frangipane

Whitaker House
1030 Hunt Valley Circle
New Kensington, PA 15068
www.whitakerhouse.com

Library of Congress Cataloging-in-Publication Data
Frangipane, Francis.
The power of one Christlike life / by Francis Frangipane.
p. cm.
Includes bibliographical references.
ISBN 0-88368-628-7
1. Christian life. I. Title.
BV4501.2 .F7143 2000
248.4—dc21   00-010957

No part of this book may be reproduced or transmitted in any form or by
any means, electronic or mechanical—including photocopying,
recording, or by any information storage and retrieval system—without
permission in writing from the publisher. Please direct your inquiries to
permissionseditor@whitakerhouse.com.

3 4 5 6 7 8 9 10 11 **ⱳ** 12 11 10 09 08 07

than 5,000 times in a year. He lived out his motto: "The world is my parish."

As stated in a monthly periodical of the 1800s, "Wesley died in perfect peace, and left a reformed nation as his monument." Surrounded by Methodist preachers and friends, Wesley was heard to say as he departed from this world, "Best of all is God is with us."

 IN CHRIST'S IMAGE TRAINING

In Christ's Image Training (ICIT), the online correspondence course Pastor Francis Frangipane has developed, is designed to train students, pastors, leaders, and intercessors to become Christlike and to release them into the power of the Lord Jesus Christ. The core curriculum includes:

§ Level I: *Certification* has four foundational tracks: Christlikeness, humility, prayer, and unity.

§ Level II: *Growing in Christ* offers further online teaching by Pastor Francis and other national church leaders covering a variety of areas, all designed to broaden the disciple's familiarity with the various graces being experienced in the body of Christ today.

§ Level III: *Facilitation and Commissioning* provides spiritual equipping for those preparing for ministerial opportunities.

The *Impartation and Focused Training* is an advanced three-day seminar offering practical, hands-on equipping that can be taken by attendance on-site or via CD/DVDs.

Please see the website for detailed information.

Note: In Christ's Image Training is not a denomination, nor is Advancing Church Ministries (ACM).

To contact the ministries of Francis Frangipane, or for equipping material, write or visit:

Advancing Church Ministries
125 Robins Square Ct.
Robins, IA 52328–9650
Toll-free order line: (877) 363-6889
www.InChristsImage.org
www.arrowbookstore.com